Business Tips

for
Personal Historians

92 Lessons Learned
from a Veteran Storyteller

DAN CURTIS

Personal History Press

Copyright © 2015 Personal History Press
All rights reserved.

ISBN 978-0-9820134-4-1 (Paperback)
ISBN 978-0-9820134-5-8 (Kindle edition)
ISBN 978-0-9820134-6-5 (Nook edition)

Edited by Kathleen McGreevy
Cover and Interior Design & Layout by Monica Lee
All rights reserved.

*For my mother, Marge Curtis,
and my partner, Jim Osborne*

Contents

FOREWORD

EDITOR'S PREFACE

INTRODUCTION 1

CHAPTER 1: THE BASICS 2

   1 3 Big Start-Up Mistakes I Made That You Can Avoid 2

   2 How to Go For the Gold in Your Business 4

   3 7 Tips on Creating a Winning Outgoing Voicemail Message 6

   4 10 Tips for Creating a Great Business Card 8

   5 Warning: Avoiding the Digital Universe
      Will Hurt Your Business 11

   6 8 Tips to Prepare Your Business for the New Year 13

   7 14 Questions to Help You Build a Better Business...........................15

   8 5 Steps to Playing a Bigger Game..17

9   16 Tips That'll Make the Most of Your Next Conference 18

10   The Introvert's Survival Guide to Conferences 21

11   6 Lessons My Cat Taught Me About Time Management 23

12   6 More "Purrfect" Business Tips from My Cat 25

13   How Can a Labyrinth Lead You to Success? 27

14   What Gardening Can Teach You
     About Growing Your Business 29

15   12 Key Tips for Successfully Working Alone 31

16   7 Ways You Can Banish Freelancer Gloom and Doom 34

Chapter 2: Becoming a Professional Personal Historian .. 37

17   The 10 Best Things About Being a Personal Historian 37

18   The 10 Worst Things About Being a Personal Historian 38

19   3 Crucial Steps to Starting Your Personal History Business 40

20   3 Things I Wish I'd Known Earlier
     About Being a Professional Personal Historian 41

21   The 3 Keys to a Successful Personal History Business 43

22   10 Commandments for the Professional Personal Historian 46

23   The Best Advice Ever for a Personal Historian 49

24   7 Indispensable Sites for the Personal Historian 52

25   12 Ways to Ensure Your Personal History Business Fails 53

26   10 Common Mistakes to Avoid When Starting
     a Personal History Business 56

27   What Makes a Personal Historian a Professional? 60

28 What You Need to Know About Becoming
    a Professional Personal Historian 61

29 What Betty White Can Teach You About Your Personal
    History Business 63

30 8 Ways to Make Your Business Stand Out From the Crowd 66

31 Do You Want To Be a Successful Personal Historian? 69

32 How to be Self-Employed and Stay Motivated 72

33 When Should You Quit Being a Personal Historian
    and Move On? 74

34 Would You Hire Yourself? 76

CHAPTER 3: GETTING & KEEPING CLIENTS 79

35 #1 Secret to Getting More Clients..79

36 3 Keys to Creating Trust with Potential Clients 81

37 7 Questions to Ask Before Taking on
    a New Personal History Client 83

38 Are You Showing Your Clients
    How Much You Appreciate Them? 86

39 Are Your Clients Extremely Satisfied With Your Service? 87

40 Are Your Clients Getting Too Little? 89

41 Guess What? Not Everyone Wants a Life Story Told 91

42 How You Can Provide a "Ritz-Carlton" Welcome
    for Potential Clients 93

43 How to Get Mom or Dad to Tell a Life Story 95

44 What Do You Do When Facing
    a Reluctant Family Storyteller? 97

45 Warning: Documenting Your Life Story Could be Fatal 100

CHAPTER 4: MARKETING & PROMOTION 102

46 The #1 Thing You Can Do to Jump Start Your Marketing......... 102

47 5 Essential Marketing Approaches for
    a Successful Personal History Business 103

48 25 No Cost or Low Cost Marketing Ideas
    for Your Personal History Business 106

49 Are You Using Storytelling to Promote
    Your Personal History Service? 109

50 5 Tips to Overcoming Your Marketing Blues................................ 112

51 8 Lessons My Mom Taught Me About Marketing....................... 114

52 Lousy at Getting Referrals? Here's Some Help. 116

53 You Can Do It! Get Referral Partners Today................................. 118

54 The Introvert's 12 Step Plan for Painless Networking................. 121

55 Attention Introverts! You Can Market Successfully!................... 124

56 10 Ways to Ensure Your Marketing Fails....................................... 126

57 What Do Fishing and Personal History Clients
    Have in Common?.. 128

58 What's the Connection Between Reflexology
    and Life Stories? 130

59 How to Ace Your Next Media Interview. 131

60 How to Get Control of Your Pre-Presentation Jitters 134

61 Should I Have a Business Blog?.. 135

62 What Everybody Ought to Know About a Successful Blog 137

63 4 Tips to Keep Your Blog Fresh, Consistent, and Enduring...... 138

64 How to Turn Your Blog Posts Into an E-Book............................ 141

65 8 Reasons Why Personal Historians Should Use Twitter 143

CHAPTER 5: WHAT I TELL PROSPECTIVE CLIENTS........................145

66 See How Easily You Can Write Your Life Story......................... 145

67 5 Benefits of Hiring a Personal Historian.................................. 146

68 How to Find a Personal Historian.. 148

69 9 Questions to Ask Before Hiring a Personal Historian............. 149

70 How Much Should You Pay a Personal Historian? 152

CHAPTER 6: DOLLARS & SENSE 155

71 Can I Make a Living as a Personal Historian? 155

72 Do You Have a Problem Knowing What to Charge Clients?..... 158

73 How to Retain Clients Who Can't Afford You............................ 160

74 How to Still be a Winner After Losing a Potential Client........... 161

75 Are You Charging Hamburger Prices for Gourmet Work? 163

76 How Much Should You Charge for a Speaking Engagement?.. 165

77 If You Don't Like What I Charge, Too Bad!................................ 168

78 Worried About Paying the Bills Between Major Projects? 169

79 16 Penny-Pinching Ideas
    to Keep Your Small Business Afloat 170

80 News Flash! Being Relaxed
    Makes People Spend More Freely 174

81 The Costliest Personal Histories in the World!........................... 177

CHAPTER 7: TAKING CARE OF YOURSELF 180

   82 How to Stop the Clock And Make Time for Yourself 180

   83 The Power of "No" 182

   84 10 Tips on Creating a Pain Free Work Space 185

   85 Creating the Spaciousness You Want in Your Life 187

   86 Stop Struggling and Succeed! 189

   87 Stop With the Productivity Pitches! 192

   88 Shut Down Your Computer! 194

   89 Are You Part of "The Great Vacationless Class?" 196

   90 The Secret to a Successful "Staycation" 198

   91 My "Staycation." Would I Do It Again? 200

   92 What Tony Bennett Can Teach Us About Burnout 201

ACKNOWLEDGMENTS 205

ABOUT THE AUTHOR 207

Foreword

FOR MANY YEARS, ABOUT the time I was starting to get clients, I was pretty much addicted to Dan Curtis's blog. It was like having a cup of tea with a friend who I really liked for his humour and humanity, except—bonus!—this friend also happened to know everything there is to know about running a personal history business. I absorbed his advice and wisdom like a sponge, and now, having seen these 92 tips, I know that even after all this time, they will continue to inspire me and help me stay on track in my personal history work—heck, in my life! I barely delivered this foreword in time because I kept losing myself reading yet another great little story that packs a big punch.

While Dan's first collection dealt with skills to do the work of a personal historian, these 92 tips focus on how to make your business a success. Naturally, a lot of that includes doing your best work, so you get the best of both worlds in this book: how to be great personal historian, and how to be marketing and business-savvy. With his signature candour, Dan writes about basic beginnings (like *3 Crucial Steps to Starting Your Personal History Business; Can I Make a Living as a Personal Historian?*);

ongoing maintenance (*How Much Should You Charge for a Speaking Engagement*; *Attention Introverts! You Can Market Successfully!*); dealing with rejection, rude clients, honestly assessing your strengths and weaknesses, and even how to design a great business card. Sometimes his tips feel like "tough love," because he doesn't mince words: *12 Ways to Ensure Your Personal History Business Fails* (watch daytime television, keep clients waiting are among the many). Sometimes they are charming and funny: *What My Cat Taught Me About Time Management*, or *What Betty White Can Teach You About Your Personal History Business*. But they all ring true and make such perfect sense, because they're rooted in the reality of Dan's own experience. I find myself nodding my head in agreement, or smiling as I remember going through the same thing.

If there's one thing personal historians have in common, it's our passion for helping people, families, business and communities tell and preserve their stories. But we come from all walks of life and probably didn't have much experience in running our own business. Starting out—getting that first client—is one thing (some would say the easy thing). Keeping it going and earning a satisfactory income is quite another. If, like me, you're in it for the long haul, you'll find you dip into this book again and again for a helping hand, a pep talk, some prodding, and good sound advice.

You'll find all that and more in these 92 tips (though all are much beefier than what you normally think of as a "tip"). This is truly an astonishing body of work that is *directly relevant* to everyday life as a personal historian. I can't imagine what a business coach would charge for all this. That Dan is sharing it for no financial gain speaks volumes about him; he has directed that proceeds from the book go to support the ongoing professional development of members of the APH. It's like having a mentor who's available any time of the day or night.

I've had the pleasure of meeting Dan and talking on the phone. He's the kind of guy you wish lived nearby so you could have him in for a cup of tea. His gentleness, sincerity, and infectious laugh would keep anyone's spirits up and be ready to take on the world—or at the very least keep doing what we love doing—and his personality shines through in this collection. Since we can't all have tea with Dan, this book is the next best thing.

—Jennifer Campbell, Owner of Heritage Memoirs and Author of *Start & Run a Personal History Business*

Editor's Preface

AFTER TEN YEARS OF experience as a personal historian, I still find myself befuddled by this or that problem having to do with owning and operating a business. Consulting Dan's book usually leads me to the answer. One day he might remind me to talk to prospective clients about investments rather than costs; another day he'll refer me to a free project management app. It's like having a business coach—one who understands all the specific needs of personal historians—by my side. Thanks, Dan!

—Kathleen McGreevy
Chapter Savers

Introduction

FOR FIVE YEARS I WROTE a professional blog for personal historians. When I began I had no idea how long it would last or that one day it would be turned into a book. I'm delighted that most of my work has now been saved and will continue to provide support to personal historians for many years to come.

This book isn't a "how to" manual. It isn't meant to be read from cover to cover. Think of it as a buffet of tasty tips rather than a four course meal. Bon appétit!

I'm pleased that all the proceeds from the sale of this book will go to support the ongoing professional development of members of the Association of Personal Historians.

CHAPTER 1:
The Basics

1 3 Big Start-Up Mistakes I Made That You Can Avoid

Thinking of giving up your current job and starting up your own business? Here are a few big mistakes I made and lessons I learned. Maybe they'll save you some anguish. Then again maybe you're smarter than I was. ;-)

In 1980 I left my job at TVOntario, an educational broadcaster, and hung up my shingle as an independent documentary filmmaker. I had a passion for documentaries, a willingness to work hard, and a creative bent. What I didn't have was two cents in my bank account. That was my first mistake.

The early years were tough. I had to borrow money from friends and get odd jobs to pay the rent and buy groceries. The effort expended on survival left little time or energy for filmmaking. Eventually I went on to be a successful documentary filmmaker but it was a lesson well learned.

Lesson 1: Don't start without money in the bank.
You'll need enough cash in hand to cover at least a year of living and business expenses. The first couple of years will be lean.

My next big mistake.

Although I was enthusiastic, I had no documentary film experience and no body of work. Few were willing to take on an eager but inexperienced filmmaker.

Lesson 2: Gain experience and have something to show potential clients.
Enthusiasm is important but clients also want to know that you can deliver. If you have little experience, highlight aspects from your previous work that indicate you can do the job.

For example, I drew on the fact that I had a Masters of Education degree. As part of that degree I had taken a course in the production and evaluation of educational media and had made a short animated film. I pointed to my work at TVOntario as a producer and as a writer of educational materials. It was a stretch but it illustrated that I was competent and had some "media" experience even if I hadn't made a documentary.

Mistake number three.

I launched into my new business with no plan, no advice, and no clear idea of what was involved in being an independent documentary filmmaker. Not something I'd recommend to others. Had I known what to expect, it could have saved me from a good deal of heartache.

Lesson 3: Have a plan. Seek advice. Know what you're getting into.

You don't need to turn this into a year-long research and development project. But tempering your enthusiasm with a little dose of reality will serve you well. Trust me!

2 How to Go For the Gold in Your Business

I've been thinking that Olympic athletes are a perfect example of what we need to do to achieve gold for our businesses. Here's how:

Goals.

Olympians are clear about their goal. They want to be the best in the world. We can't achieve the results we want in our businesses unless we aim to be the best. What do you need to do right now to achieve your best?

Training.

World-class athletes continually train and push themselves to the limit and beyond. As small business owners we need to do the same. What are the skills you need to perfect? What's working for you and what has to be dropped? How do you push yourself to the limit?

Coaching.

Athletes can't do it all on their own. They rely on coaches to help them develop their skills. There are business and personal coaches who can do the same for you. What's stopping you from hiring a coach? What do you need to do to overcome that obstacle?

Perseverance.

Elite athletes have setbacks but they don't give up. Operating a small business can be tough at times. We encounter challenges that can be discouraging. But if we want to go for the gold we have to pick ourselves up and keep going. What is your biggest challenge right now? How can you surmount it?

Competition.

Competing with others pushes athletes to achieve their best. Look at those businesses that offer similar products and services as yours. What competing businesses do you really admire? How can you do better?

Concentration.

Watching an Olympian in motion is to see someone with exquisite concentration. In our businesses we have to be similarly focused. How can you be more focused in your work? What do you need to give up to achieve concentration?

Balance.

World-class athletes know that they must balance their hard work with rest, good diet, and friends and family. When you're running a small business, it's easy to go non-stop. How's your work/life balance right now? What can you do to achieve a more balanced life?

3 7 Tips on Creating a Winning Outgoing Voicemail Message

Have you listened to your outgoing voicemail message lately? Does it sound professional? Like someone you'd want to do business with? If not, you could be losing potential clients. Here's what you need to do:

1. Avoid old answering machines with poor quality audio.

What kind of business impression do you create if your prospective caller can hardly make out your voicemail message because of static and a barely audible voice? If I were hiring you to do a video or audio recording, I'd have second thoughts!

Be smart. Use a telephone company answering service or a good quality digital answering machine.

2. Make it clear as to the person the caller has reached.

You might say something like, "Thank you for calling. You've reached the voicemail of Kathy Smith, owner of Lifestory Productions."

Don't leave an announcement like, "Hi, I'm not in. Please leave a message after the tone." Callers have no idea if they've reached the correct number or if their message will actually reach the right person.

3. Leave instructions.

Many voicemail messages end with something like "Please leave your name and number after the beep." It's a start. But if all you get is, "Hi, this is Bob call me at 200-4000," you have a problem. Who is Bob and what does he want? Does this call require immediate attention?

A better outgoing message provides the caller with some guidance. Here's a sample: "Please leave your name, the reason for your call, a number where you can be reached, and the best time for me to call you."

4. Be concise.

Callers don't want to listen to a lengthy monologue before they can leave a message. Your voicemail announcement shouldn't be more than 20 seconds long.

5. Avoid being cute and clever.

Even if you have the wit of a Mark Twain, cleverness can wear thin if a caller is hearing your message for the third time. Keep it simple and business-like.

6. Script and rehearse your message.

We've all heard voicemail messages that covered the spectrum from flat and bored to breathless and rushed.

The tone of your voice is as important as the words being spoken. I once worked with an actress on some narration for a documentary of mine. At one point she said, "I can do that line with a smile in my voice. It'll work better." She was right. She actually spoke the line while smiling. It sounded friendly and welcoming.

Begin by writing down what you want to say. Read it aloud. Edit your message until it sounds right. Now try it on a friend or family member and get a critique. Before recording your message do several rehearsals so that you can deliver your lines flawlessly and with a smile in your voice.

7. Record your message in a quiet environment.

Nothing reeks more of amateurishness than a voicemail message with a background cacophony of dogs barking, kids screaming, and TVs blaring. Find a quiet room to record, preferably one with lots of sound absorbing material like a bedroom.

And finally...

Here's a sample of an outgoing message that you can adapt to suit your needs.

> *"Hello. You've reached the voicemail of Kathy Smith, owner of Lifestory Productions. Please leave your name, telephone number, the reason for your call, and the best time for me to reach you. Thanks for calling."*

4 | 10 Tips for Creating a Great Business Card

Dollar for dollar, your business card is one of your best forms of advertising. I've been looking at my card lately and thinking it's time for a major makeover. It's not that it's terrible. It's just not memorable. So I've been doing a little research on what makes for a great card. I've distilled it down to these ten key points:

1. Include only essential contact information.

This means your name and principal contact number. Don't include a fax or a cell number or address if you rarely use these for business.

2. Keep your card clean and clutter free.

You want it to be easy to read. Clutter is confusing and conveys a sense of disorganization and poor design sense.

3. Don't print your cards on your home office printer.

You simply can't get the same quality card stock as a professional printer and your cards will feel cheap. That's not something you want to convey.

4. Make your design reflect your business.

Put what you do on your card. For personal historians, you don't want cartoon characters in neon glow colors. That would be fine for an animation studio. Think legacy, books, film, memories, families, passing time, love….anything that suggests the work we do.

5. Show your personality.

You want your card to be memorable. Add a dash of color and an image that says something about you. Perhaps you could include a studio portrait of yourself or an image that conveys your style.

6. Add a tag line.

Create something that's short and memorable. I'm thinking of using what I coined for my brochure, *Preserving Memories Is an Act of Love*.

7. Make it readable.

It's surprising how many people put light type on a white background or dark type on a darker background. Don't use italicized or script fonts. They're hard to read. If people have to squint to read your card, you've lost them.

8. Leave your card back blank.

Some argue that it makes sense to use every inch of your card. Others believe that a blank back gives you room to add more information or space for people to make a note about you. I'm for the blank back.

9. Keep the standard format.

Offbeat formats may be clever and fun but they're hard to store and too often get trashed. If you can afford it, a slight variation on the standard is to have one curved end or rounded corners. It's a classy look.

10. Hire a graphic designer.

It can be expensive but the results are worth it. Business cards are a design challenge. To creatively convey information, style, and values—all in a memorable wallet size card—is not a job for amateurs.

Check out these books for more inspiration:

- *It's in the Cards.* "Ivan Misner, Candace Bailly and Dan Georgevich review more than 2,000 business cards from 10 countries and select more than 200 examples of some of the best, which are shown throughout the book in full-color."
- *The Best of the Best of Business Card Design (Graphic Design)* "…readers will find hundreds of unique and memorable designs in a broad range of colors, styles, and shapes for every type of client. Filled with inspiration for designers and their clients, this creative resource shows how any individual or business can make a tiny space speak volumes about who they are and what they do."
- *The Business Card Book.* "This comprehensive book contains all the information you need to create an effective business card. It is

divided into four parts: deciding what messages you want to communicate; crafting a powerful card; using your card to build business; finding useful resources and references."

5 Warning: Avoiding the Digital Universe Will Hurt Your Business

Let me begin by saying there are legitimate reasons to be wary of the ever-expanding digital universe—a glut of junk information, loss of privacy, time wasting, and addiction. But there are also irrational fears at work based in part on our inherent resistance to change.

Change happens. And a good thing too. Lucky for us there was the invention of the printing press. Monks no longer toil on illuminated texts for a select few. Manual typewriters have a certain aesthetic appeal but quite frankly I was happy to throw out the rolls of correction tape.

> *Computers in the future may weigh no more than 1.5 tons.* ~ Popular Mechanics, 1949

There are those for whom the world was a much better place when we read "real" books, wrote in longhand, and used manual typewriters. There's a wistful longing for a slower paced, more genteel life. And while I sympathize, I can't help but feel that these people are missing a richness of experience that's just a click away.

> *Television won't matter in your lifetime or mine.*
> ~ Richard Lambert, broadcaster, 1936

If you're not running a small business, it probably doesn't matter if you're digitally savvy. But if you want to create a successful personal history business, you've got to stick more than your big toe into the digital stream. This doesn't mean you have to be sucked under and drown. But it does mean that you need to be familiar with what's out there to be able to pick and choose the digital tools that'll help your business. Sticking your head in the sand and ignoring the wealth of resources that are available will hurt your business.

Here are a few digital resources worth considering.

- *E-books:* add a whole innovative and interactive realm to life stories with text, videos, photos, maps, documents, and more.
- *Webinars:* increase marketing reach using such services as *GoToMeeting*.
- *Blogging:* build conversations and credibility with clients using a free service such as *WordPress* or *Blogger*.
- *VoIP:* extend interviewing reach world-wide with a service such as *Skype*.
- *Podcasting:* reach a wider audience with information and support using such services as *BlogTalkRadio*.
- *Video ads:* run ads in videos with *Google's AdSense*.
- *Booklets:* turn a PDF file into a handy information booklet using *bookcreator.com*.
- *POD:* print a sample copy of a book using a print-on-demand service such as *CreateSpace*.
- *QR Codes:* print these codes on your business cards and send clients to a URL site where they can access more information

about your services, get discount coupons, access video, and more. You can create a QR Code at http://goqr.me/.

- *Desktop publishing:* design books, flyers, brochures, and posters with such programs as *InDesign* and *Microsoft Publisher.*
- *Project management:* find a list of 10 free project Management applications at http://freelancefolder.com/10-free-project-management-applications/.

6 8 Tips to Prepare Your Business for the New Year

Your small business is like your car. It needs regular servicing to keep it running smoothly.

With the year rapidly drawing to a close, now's the time to give your business a tune-up. Here are 8 tips that'll have your company running like a Rolls Royce in the New Year.

1. Evaluate

Take a hard look at what's not working in your business and drop it. It might be a marketing approach that has failed to generate leads. Or it might be fees that are too low to sustain your business.

Similarly, look at what's working. How can you do more or improve on your success? Maybe your speaking engagements have been a great way of getting new clients. Consider offering more.

2. De-clutter

Finding it hard to find the surface of your desk? Are there file folders and books stacked on the floor? Actually, it's beginning to sound a lot like my office. ;-)

You'll feel more organized and on top of things once you get rid of extraneous stuff. You don't have to be a fanatic about it. A little order and spaciousness can go a long way. Set aside a few minutes a day and you'll be surprised how much you can accomplish. Just to let you know, I've started my own de-cluttering. I do have a desk!

3. Bookkeeping

If you keep your receipts in a shoebox, it's time to consider a bookkeeper or an accounting software program.

It's critical that you have a clear picture of income, expenses, and profit. Without an ongoing snapshot of your financials you'll never be able to accurately assess your company's health.

4. Learn

Being a successful small business owner requires constantly upgrading and learning new skills. Look for webinars, tutorials, expert speakers, and courses that will make a difference to your performance in the year ahead.

5. Connect

There's a wealth of information and support to be found in professional and small business associations. For example, if you're a personal historian and haven't yet joined the Association of Personal Historians (www.personalhistorians.org), make sure to join today.

6. Plan

Without a road map you'll never know where you're going. Look ahead at the coming year and write down your goals. Keep them realistic. Grandiose plans are sure to fail and will leave you discouraged.

For some excellent help, check out *Really Simple Goal Setting* (http://zenhabits.net/really-simple-goal-setting/).

7. Website

If you don't have a website or blog, get one. If you have one, it's time to take a critical look at it. How fresh is the content? How easy is it to navigate around the site? What's missing? What can be discarded? How professional does it look?

8. Self-care

A healthy business needs a healthy owner. It's easy to neglect your own care when working hard to make a success of your business.

Make certain to schedule time for you in your day planner. Whether it's going to the gym or for a walk, meditating or reading a book, you need to give yourself permission to relax and recharge.

7 14 Questions to Help You Build a Better Business

I find the end of the year a good time to take stock of my personal history business. I set aside a day and look at my successes and the things that didn't work. I make a point of writing this all down.

It's an important exercise that holds me accountable and keeps me growing as a professional. Why not take some time and do your own year-end review?

A word of caution: Don't beat yourself up for perceived failures but at the same time don't sweep them under the rug. Here are the questions I ask myself. What questions would you add?

1. What has worked this year?
2. Why has it worked?
3. What have I learned from my successes?
4. How will I apply this learning to next year?
5. What hasn't worked this year?
6. Why hasn't it worked?
7. What have I learned from my failures?
8. How will I apply this learning to next year?
9. What do I need to do more of?
10. What do I need to do less of?
11. On a scale of 1 to 10, how satisfied am I with my performance this year?
12. What do I need to do to push my satisfaction level higher?
13. Where do I want to be at this time next year?
14. What do I have to do to get there?

8 5 Steps to Playing a Bigger Game

There's a tendency for us to play small when we're frightened by both recessionary times and shrinking bank accounts. It's natural to want to pull up the drawbridge and hunker down. But if we're not careful, we become habitual small thinkers and our dreams wither and die. What would it take for you to play a bigger game?

Here are five steps that will get you to think big.

1. Silence your Inner Gremlin.

Our Gremlins are those critical inner voices that try to keep us firmly rooted in the status quo. As soon as you think about playing a bigger game, they start harassing you. "Who do you think you are? You don't have enough experience to do that. What will people think? You'll probably fail." You need to recognize your Gremlin voices and firmly tell them to "get lost." If you need some help, I highly recommend the book *Taming Your Gremlin*.

2. Step out of your comfort zone.

We're drawn to comfort and it can smother us. The truth is that nothing comes from playing it safe. One of the biggest stumbling blocks to playing a bigger game is not stepping out of your comfort zone and taking risks. It's scary to do so. Ask yourself, what's the absolute worst thing that could happen? Now hold that scenario in your mind and ask yourself if you could handle this worst case. The chances are you'll probably answer, "Yes!"

3. Organize support.

You'll need to find people who share your dream. Your support group can be drawn from friends, colleagues, and personal coaches. They'll be there to give you feedback, ask powerful questions, and help keep you focused on your vision.

4. Ask yourself the right questions.

In order to be clear about where you are and where you want to be, ask yourself:

- How am I playing small?
- What do I yearn for?
- What's holding me back?
- What do I need to do to move forward?

5. Take action.

If you spend all your time reflecting, reading, and analyzing but never putting your plan into action, you'll have failed. This is where your support group is invaluable. They can hold you accountable and keep you focused on your dream.

9 16 Tips That'll Make the Most of Your Next Conference

Going to a conference is a major commitment of time and money. You want to make the most of it. Here are some tips that will help.

Before the conference:

1. *Do your homework.* Select the names of people you'd like to meet. Use Twitter, Facebook, and Google to get some background information on the speakers and workshop presenters. E-mail those you want to connect with and set up times when you can get together. A word of advice: Don't try to talk to keynote speakers after their presentations because you'll only end up in a throng of other attendees.

2. *Choose your workshops.* It makes sense to select sessions that you absolutely don't want to miss. What I've found though is that it's also fun to stretch yourself and attend a workshop that exposes you to some different content and ideas. Be open to possibilities.

3. *Pack clothes for layering.* Conference venues can be notoriously too hot or too cold so have clothes that can be easily pulled on or shed.

4. *Pack an extra light bag.* You'll inevitably pick up stuff and you'll need space to haul it home.

5. *Pack your business essentials.* This includes business cards, pens, your laptop, and a notebook. Don't forget to bring a sample of your work. You may meet a potential client.

6. *Find out about your conference destination.* Take time to learn something about the host city.

At the conference:

1. *Arrive early or stay late.* If possible, extend your visit by a day. You've spent hard earned money and traveled some distance to get to your conference. Don't waste the opportunity to explore your host city and environs. You may not get there again.

2. *Familiarize yourself with the conference center.* Nothing wastes more time than floundering around the first day trying to find where you're going. Before the conference starts, take your conference map and locate the venues for the workshops you'll be attending. Make a note of washrooms, bookstores, and coffee break locations.

3. *Don't miss the keynote presentations.* These are designed to be stimulating and thought-provoking. You'll also have something in common to share with other attendees.

4. *Stay healthy.* It's easy to indulge in too much food and drink, not to mention the hours spent sitting. This saps your energy and lowers your immune system. Take time to go for a run or walk. Conferences, especially in the winter, are a breeding ground for germs. Make sure to wash your hands frequently and carry some antiseptic towelettes.

5. *Network.* For my fellow introverts this can sometimes be a challenge. And yet one of the best reasons for going to a conference is to meet others. So if you haven't, read *The Introvert's Survival Guide to Conferences* (10) and then step up to the plate. You'll make lasting friendships, develop invaluable business connections, and learn a whole bunch of useful stuff.

6. *Leave a session that doesn't have value for you.* If after 15 minutes you feel your time is not being well spent, get up and leave. That's why I like to sit near the door so I can make a speedy exit. Always have another session in mind that you can drop into... late. I know it's hard not to feel like you're being rude. But remember you're not at the conference to make presenters happy.

7. Keep a conference diary. Every day prepare notes on people, ideas, action steps, and insights. It's hard to remember everything if you leave it until you get home.

8. Have fun. Make sure to attend social functions and planned outings. Take in some local sites by yourself or with a conference buddy. Do yourself a favor and make these "non-business" outings. Don't see this as yet another opportunity to network.

9. Ask questions. Speak up. If you don't understand something in a session or want more information, don't be afraid to blurt out your questions. No question is silly or unimportant. Repeat this mantra many times. ;-)

10. Consider shipping home your conference "acquisitions." Rather than haul extra books, conference manuals, and gifts back with you, make arrangements to have them couriered. It'll save your back and make your return trip more enjoyable.

10 The Introvert's Survival Guide to Conferences

I love people, but I must admit I can't be around them continually. It drains me. Hello, my name is Dan and I'm an introvert.

I previously wrote *Attention Introverts! You Can Market Successfully!* (55) Now I'd like to turn my attention to another challenge for introverts—conferences. If the thought of spending days submerged in a sea of people is daunting, don't despair. This article is for you.

- *Make space for downtime.* By all means, attend all the workshops and keynote events that look interesting. But don't fill your day with wall-to-wall events. Escape to your hotel room for an hour to read, nap, or just stare into space. I find going for a walk outside helps recharge my batteries.

- *Avoid a hotel roommate.* The last thing you need is to have the stress of dealing with a roommate when you just want to relax. If you're budget-minded and plan to share, here's my advice. Make every effort to find a fellow introvert. Or failing that, at least someone you know who can respect your need for quiet.

- *Exit conversations gracefully.* It might be at a coffee break, meal, or in the hallway, but there'll be times you need to escape from yet another conversation. Make sure you have a few handy exit lines to draw on such as "I'm sorry, but I need some time to freshen up before the next workshop." "I'm sorry, but I have a call I need to make." "I promised to meet up with someone and I need to find them. You'll have to excuse me."

- *Make meaningful connections.* I find I'm at my best one-on-one. I make it a point to prepare a list of a few key people I want to see at a conference. Then I set up appointments with those individuals to meet over a coffee or drinks.

- *Have a conference "extrovert" buddy.* This can be a friend, colleague, or someone you meet at the conference. Extroverts love meeting new people and can be the perfect partner at mixers and parties. They'll introduce you to all kinds of people. No need to stand in the shadows!

- *Consider an "off site" spot or room service for a meal.* I'm not one to enjoy my breakfast with a cast of hundreds. When I can, I look for a nearby cheap and cheerful café to get away from the crowds.

Treat yourself to the occasional meal out or room service. It'll do wonders for your soul.

11 6 Lessons My Cat Taught Me About Time Management

My cat Annie is full of useful lessons. And for those of you who say that lack of time is keeping you from getting your life story told, here's what Annie knows about good time management.

1. Decide what's important and drop the rest.

There's always time to do the important things. Annie has clear priorities—sleeping, eating, observing, playing, and snuggling. Anything else is of little interest to her and she doesn't do it. Take a moment and make a list of things you have to do today. Now put an "A" beside the absolute must-do items. Drop the rest. This may sound drastic but you can't humanly tackle everything you think needs doing in a day.

2. Learn to say "No."

Ever try to convince a cat to do something it doesn't want to do? It's taken me a while to do what Annie does really well, and that's to say "No" and not feel guilty about it. No is a very powerful word. It helps you set boundaries and drop those time-sucking activities.

3. Concentrate on one thing at a time.

Annie never multitasks. She's wise, because studies show it doesn't work.

4. Reward yourself.

Annie has learned that good behavior, like coming when I whistle for her, comes with a small treat. It reinforces good habits I want to instill in her. When you've completed a difficult task make sure you give yourself a treat—maybe a good bottle of wine or fine chocolate truffles.

5. Establish routines and stick with them.

Annie is a creature of habit. She thrives on routine. She expects me up at 6 am to feed her. While my porridge cooks, we have a ten-minute playtime. This is usually followed by her first outing of the day. If we know how our day is structured, we can better fine-tune it to meet the demands that arise.

6. Start your day right.

Annie has a good breakfast followed by 30 minutes of meditation. For some reason she loves to curl up with me as I do my daily Vipassana Meditation. If you're too rushed to find a moment of calm in the morning, the chances are you'll start your day stressed. This in turn will lead to poor decision-making and ineffective use of your time.

While we can't create more hours in a day, we can manage our time so that we create the space we need for those important projects, like our life story. What are you doing to manage your time more effectively?

12 6 More "Purrfect" Business Tips from My Cat

Groan. Don't you just hate puns?

Anyhow, my cat Annie is a source of inspiration for my life and business. In a previous article, I shared *6 Lessons My Cat Taught Me About Time Management* (11). I might add, she was quite pleased by the positive response that article received!

Here are some more of Annie's pearls of wisdom.

1. Take time to play.
Every day Annie insists we play at least once if not twice. If I'm not available, she'll make up her own games. She'll race madly about the house, dive into a stack of newspapers, or climb the plum tree. She knows the wisdom of the old saying "All work and no play makes…" Make certain to build play time into your daily schedule.

2. Exercise caution in any new situation.
Annie doesn't immediately take to new things. A new chair, plant, or visitor is carefully and gingerly approached, sniffed, and either tentatively accepted or rejected until she feels more comfortable.

Whenever you embark on a new project or work with a new client, you could emulate her behavior (well maybe not the sniffing part). Take time to do your homework and assess the situation before plunging in.

3. Claim your territory.
Annie has claimed the backyard as her territory. She defends it vigorously from other cats. And for the most part they now leave her

alone. It's important to claim your space in the business world. Be clear on what you're offering and to whom. Then stand up and stand out!

4. Be curious.

All cats love to explore. And Annie's no exception. In the summer she spends hours in the backyard, peering into flowerbeds and checking out the next door neighbor's yard. She comes in at the end of the day, tired and stimulated.

Curiosity is a tonic that keeps your business fresh and relevant. Be curious about your competition, potential new products and services, and interesting marketing ideas.

5. Be gentle but strong.

Annie is petite, soft, and gentle. That is until she feels threatened by another cat. Then she puffs herself up to twice her size and lets out a blood-curdling scream. It seldom goes any further than that. The other cat receives the message and retreats. I'm not suggesting you puff yourself up and start screaming at people who upset you. Even though this might satisfy the "inner cat" in you! What I am saying is that you must be clear that you will not be taken advantage of or treated poorly. Stand up for your rights!

6. Break the pattern.

Annie's a creature of routine. She has her favorite chair and set times for eating. She loves a snuggle while I'm watching a little TV at night. But she also mixes it up. She'll decide to move to a different spot to sleep or skip the snuggle and be on her own. It's useful in our business to avoid becoming stale by doing the same thing over and over again. Follow Annie's example and change things now and again.

Annie has looked this article over and approved its content. Whew! She can be so demanding.

13 How Can a Labyrinth Lead You to Success?

> *If you don't know where you're going, you might not get there.* —Yogi Berra

Recently I walked a labyrinth. I don't do this regularly. But I was attending a silent weekend Buddhist retreat and outside the retreat center was a large labyrinth.

You can find business lessons almost anywhere.

I became aware that walking the labyrinth was akin to establishing and running a successful personal history business. There is a beginning with all the anticipation of the journey ahead. And there's an end goal of a flourishing business. And the distance between these two points is not a straight line but a series of intricate interconnecting paths.

What does a labyrinth have to teach us about running a successful personal history business?

Have a plan.

You need to know where you're going and how to get there.

In a labyrinth, just as you're about to reach your destination, the path veers off and you find yourself moving away. But you trust if you keep following it, you'll eventually reach your goal. And you do.

Similarly, in your personal history business you need to have a clearly marked path. It starts with having in place a workable business plan that will give you confidence to get through the inevitable twists and turns your business will take.

Don't give up.

Like the twisting path of the labyrinth, you'll encounter setbacks in your business. It's easy to get discouraged. But if you have a solid business plan and are committed to reaching your goal, then you'll be encouraged to continue, knowing that success can be yours.

Take time for reflection.

Walking a labyrinth is in part an exercise in reflection. The mind is focused on the path, allowing some of the busyness of your life to settle. You can see more clearly.

Running your personal history business can seem overwhelming at times. There's so much to do and so little time to do it. But successful business owners take time to examine where their company has been, where it's going, and what changes need to be made to keep on track.

Make time to reflect on the health of your business.

Conclusion.

Having a sound and wise path to follow in life and in business is the trick to happiness. There is no one path. You'll need to determine what's right for you. Once you've chosen your path, set out with joy, courage, and humbleness.

And remember what Yogi Berra said:

> *"If you don't know where you're going, you might not get there."*

14 What Gardening Can Teach You About Growing Your Business

Do you want your business to grow? Then why not apply some basic gardening know-how to your enterprise?

1. Choose appropriate plants.

Experienced gardeners know that to grow the healthiest plants they need to select varieties that suit the local climate. How do you select your clients?

Aim your marketing at those who need your service. There's no point in wasting time and money going after clients who have little interest in your product or service. Take the time to research carefully who your potential clients are and where you're likely to find them. If you're a personal historian, one of your client groups will be older people wanting to leave a legacy for their children or grandchildren. Another group will likely be parents who want a record of Grandma or Grandpa's story to pass on to their children.

2. Fertilize.

Every garden needs an appropriate amount of good organic fertilizer to replenish the soil and ensure long-term growth. What are you doing to fertilize your business? What would you add to my list?

- *Conferences.* A good conference is invigorating. It connects you to new people and ideas.
- *Courses and workshops.* These are great ways to learn how to enhance your business skills.
- *Downtime.* It can be a mini-break in the day for exercise or meditation or a longer absence such as a vacation or sabbatical. Whatever you decide, downtime is an important way to nourish you and your business.
- *Networking.* Getting out and meeting people is one of the tried and true methods of growing your business.

3. Dig out the weeds.

If you let the weeds overrun your garden, they soon sap the strength of your plants and in some cases kill them. What weeds are growing in your business? What others would you add to my list?

- *clients from hell*
- *unorganized filing systems*
- *time-sucking distractions like daytime TV or social networking*
- *lethargy*
- *scattered or non-existent marketing plans*

The Basics

4. Water.

Not all plants need the same amount of water. Over or under-watering can be the downfall of many a gardener. Here are some examples of over-watering or under-watering a business. What are your examples?

- *Over-watering.* Overwhelming potential clients with too much marketing, e.g. fliers, e-mails, telephone solicitations, and newsletters.
- *Under-watering.* Failure to acknowledge the person who sent you a referral or not sending former clients a greeting at special times of the year like Christmas or birthdays.

With patience and good gardening practices you can better your chances of growing a flourishing business. How's your garden growing?

15 12 Key Tips for Successfully Working Alone

I've been self-employed for more years than I can recall. I've loved being my own boss. But it hasn't been all sunshine and roses. There have been some real challenges and some hard slogging. Over time I've learned some things about working alone and I'd like to share them with you.

1. Create a home office.

It's important to keep your overhead down so don't spend money on an outside office. Make sure your home office is a place where you can work without being disturbed. Close the door. The sound of barking dogs and crying children isn't very professional when you're on the phone with clients. It's also important to make a clear mental separation between the place where you live and the place where you work in your home.

2. Get a comfortable ergonomic chair.
One of my best investments was a quality ergonomic chair. You'll be spending many hours in your chair. You want to be comfortable and properly supported so that you don't end your day with aching muscles.

3. Set work hours.
The quickest route to failure is to wander through your workday without any sense of a beginning or end to it. You don't need to punch in at 9 a.m., but you do need to be disciplined about when you start. Make certain to have a fixed time of the day when you stop work. Don't keep pushing on until midnight.

4. Look sharp.
Get out of your PJs and bathrobe. It might be tempting to shuffle around in your rabbit slippers but it doesn't instill a sense of professionalism. You don't need to put on a suit but you do need to change into something that makes you feel sharp.

5. Enlist the services of a bookkeeper.
You need to set up a bookkeeping system to get a handle on your income and expenses. Hire a person who is familiar with the needs of the self-employed.

6. Get insurance.
Speak to an insurance broker to assess whether your home insurance adequately covers your home-based business.

7. Be persistent.

I like to remark that I'm not brilliant but I'm persistent! When I look back, I realize that I've accomplished a good deal because I seldom gave up unless it was clearly a futile exercise. To succeed on your own, you have to keep pushing ahead through the inevitable setbacks and roadblocks.

8. Join a business networking group.

Isolation can be a detrimental factor when working alone. Find out what local business networking groups are in your area and join one or two of them.

9. Have passion for your work.

One of the challenges of working on your own is that you don't necessarily have "cheerleaders" to keep you motivated. If you don't absolutely love what you're doing, it will become increasingly difficult to get through the hard times.

10. Don't be consumed by work.

It's easy to go non-stop when you're working alone. Make sure to take 10 or 15 minute breaks every hour. Schedule time for family and friends. Go for a brisk walk.

11. Prepare a list.

You need to have a plan for your day. It can be something simple like writing down the three things you must complete today. I like to use the *GTD* approach (http://gettingthingsdone.com/) to maintaining productivity. It helps to break big tasks into manageable pieces.

12. Keep learning.

This is critical because you need to keep on top of changing technologies and trends. Find time to take training programs and workshops, read books, subscribe to newsletters, and attend lectures.

16. 7 Ways You Can Banish Freelancer Gloom and Doom

No clients knocking on your door? Feeling discouraged? Thinking of quitting?

I've been there and know what that feels like. It's no fun. So what can you do to get through the gloom and doom?

Here are a few things I've learned along the way.

Accept.

Things happen—both good and bad. That's life. Accept the fact that as grim as your present situation is, it will change.

When you catch yourself listening to the voices of gloom and doom nattering in your head, switch channels. Your thoughts are just thoughts. They're not solid objects. Just let them pass without becoming caught up in them.

Reflect.

Take some time to examine your intentions.

What were your intentions when you started your freelance business? Was it to make a lot of money? Serve your community? Supplement your income? How have your intentions changed? Do changed intentions require you to re-evaluate your marketing approach? Maybe your intentions are different and you no longer have the same passion that you started with.

Stepping back and examining your intentions may provide a clue to your present dilemma.

Avoid.

Looking at colleagues who are successful can lead to feelings of envy or incompetence. Likewise, identifying with others who are struggling like yourself can be demoralizing. You begin to think, "Why bother? It's all hopeless."

The quickest way to spiral into gloom and doom is to compare yourself to others. Avoid comparisons.

Revitalize.

Close the door to your office, disconnect from your beeping electronic devices, and indulge in things that bring you real joy. Forget about your business for a couple of weeks. It'll still be there when you get back.

Returning to your work after a complete break gives you more energy and gives you fresh insights into your business.

Connect.

We all need support.

Thinking that you can do it all on your own is a recipe for disaster. Make sure you connect with people who can provide practical advice, a shoulder to cry on, and inspiration.

Persevere.

No one said it would be easy establishing a new business. Overnight success rarely happens. Unrealistic expectations about your success will inevitably lead to disappointment and doubt.

Be prepared for the long haul. It'll take a couple of years of hard work before you begin to see the fruits of your labor. Knowing this will help keep you from despair when times are tough.

Laugh.

Last but not least, laugh more! Some days the old saying, "If I didn't laugh, I'd cry" sums it up. We need to lighten up. Grim determination and a furrowed brow won't make work easier.

CHAPTER 2:
Becoming a Professional Personal Historian

17 The 10 Best Things About Being a Personal Historian

Some of you might be considering the plunge into being a full time professional personal historian. I've been at this work for several years now and I thought it might be of help if I told you what I love about it. In Tip 18 I'll tell you the worst things about being a personal historian. But for now here's the good stuff!

1. You get to learn from people who have a lifetime of rich and fascinating stories.
2. You have the opportunity to be involved with a supportive and creative group of fellow personal historians.

3. You can spend a good amount of your work time at home. No commuting.

4. You make a valuable contribution to the preservation of a family's history.

5. You are your own boss. You get to set the agenda.

6. There's plenty of opportunity for you to learn and grow professionally.

7. Having clients reflect on their lives makes you more reflective.

8. You have the great satisfaction that comes from watching the look of delight on the faces of your clients as they view, for the first time, their completed book or video.

9. You are involved in work that is nurturing, peaceful, life enhancing, and soul satisfying.

10. You make it possible for future generations to hear the voice and share in the wisdom of a long departed family member.

18 The 10 Worst Things About Being a Personal Historian

In Tip 17, I wrote about the ten things that I liked best about being a professional personal historian. Now to be honest, this work has its challenges. I'm not trying to discourage anyone and at the same time I think it's wise to go into something new with your eyes wide open. Would anything on the following list make you reconsider a career as a personal historian?

1. Minimal income at the start. Until you've built up a client base, your revenues will be slim for at least a couple of years. I speak from experience.
2. No regular paycheck. If you've been a salaried employee, it can be a shock to suddenly find there's no check at the end of the week.
3. An uneven workflow. It can often be a question of feast or famine—too many clients or too few.
4. Working alone. You can spend days and weeks on your own. Now for some this may be a benefit not a handicap.
5. Marketing your services. If you're an introvert like me, this can be a challenge. But if you don't market your services, you won't get clients and your business will fail.
6. Inconsiderate clients. Most are a pleasure to work with. And then I've had a few potential clients who never return calls. This, after I've spent time with them working out a personalized life story package and budget. It's annoying. Other personal historians can attest to their own "clients from hell."
7. Little free time. If you want to earn the income you feel you need, you'll find yourself putting in long days and long weeks. Being self-employed and successful is hard work especially if you're trying to balance it with domestic responsibilities.
8. Working in a profession that is unregulated. Anyone can claim to be a personal historian—there's no certification or governing body. For the potential client this can create confusion. Some personal historians have years of experience and others none. Some charge very little while others charge thousands of dollars. A potential client can well question why they should pay me a

professional rate when someone down the street is offering a bargain basement fee.

9. Keeping up with changing technologies. An example: A few years ago I invested a few thousand dollars into the latest 3-chip, mini-DV prosumer camcorder. It's now obsolete because it doesn't shoot in HD and isn't flash-based. I can still get some use out of my camcorder but I will eventually have to upgrade.

10. If you don't do it, it won't get done. It's not always practical or easy to delegate some tasks. So for most of us it means wearing many different hats. In any one day you can be a marketer, bookkeeper, writer, editor, event planner, interviewer, and administrative assistant. While this can be a lot of fun, it can also be stressful and lead to burn out.

19 3 Crucial Steps to Starting Your Personal History Business

How should you start your new business? I know this is going to sound heretical but forget the business plans, brochures, business cards, and website. All that stuff can come later. Believe me. Here's what you need to do right now.

1. Talk to some professional personal historians.
When I started out, I found a personal historian in my community who had been doing this work for fifteen years. I spent an afternoon picking her brain. She was gracious with her time and advice. Talking to experienced personal historians will provide you with invaluable start-

up help. To find a personal historian go the *Association of Personal Historians* website and click on the *Find a Personal Historian* tab.

2. Produce a life story book or video.

Start with a friend or relative. Even if you've already done this for a family member, don't miss this step. It's crucial. You need a portfolio you can show prospective clients and you need experience. What you'll want to do is keep a very detailed record of the time you spend on each and every phase of the project. This will be useful information in determining the fees you'll need to charge. Also keep a journal of the things that are working, not working, surprises, and questions you need answered.

3. Reflect on your experience.

After you've completed your personal history project, go back and read through the journal you wrote. Reflect on your experience and ask yourself these three questions: Was this a good experience for me? Am I excited about starting work on another life story? Am I prepared to put in the hard work to make a success of this new endeavor? If you can enthusiastically answer "Yes!" to these three questions, you're well on your way. Congratulations!

20 3 Things I Wish I'd Known Earlier About Being a Professional Personal Historian

Want to avoid some pitfalls as a newcomer to the personal history business? Read on.

We love our work. Right? But that doesn't mean we can't be blindsided by some unsuspected snag. Looking back on my seven years in this work there are a number of things I wish I'd known earlier. Here are just three:

1. Some personal history clients can be darn right disagreeable.

It's true, and I have the scars to prove it.

For the most part, working with people on a personal history project is a satisfying experience. That's why early on I was lulled into a dream-like state, believing all my clients would be simply wonderful. Wrong! One "client from hell" snapped me out of my reverie.

What did I learn? I now make sure that I only work with clients that are a good fit and that I like. In addition, I'm very clear from the outset about what I will or won't do. And I always make certain clients sign a contract.

2. Keeping up with changing technologies never stops.

A few years ago I invested several thousand dollars in the latest prosumer camcorder. It was a beauty. Now it's obsolete. It doesn't shoot in HD and isn't flash-based. I'll soon have to purchase a new camera that will also necessitate an upgrade of my editing software.

It's not just keeping up with the latest equipment and software. You've also got to budget for these upgrades. I'm embarrassed to admit that in this department I've been somewhat lax.

What's the lesson? Build into your production budget a rental fee for your equipment. Make sure that those fees go into a designated new equipment fund. And keep repeating to yourself: "This too will soon be obsolete."

3. Working in an unregulated profession has its disadvantages.

There's no certification or governing body for personal historians. Some are experienced veterans and others are just starting out. Some charge nothing or very little while others charge thousands of dollars. For potential clients this can be confusing. They may well ask why they should pay you a professional fee when someone down the street is offering a bargain basement deal.

What's the answer? I've learned not to sell myself short and not to be "nickel and dimed" to death. I sell myself on my years of experience as an award winning documentary filmmaker. I promise a professionally produced personal history that my clients will be thrilled with or they get their money back. If they still prefer to go with "Joe" down the street and are happy with a less qualified person and an inferior product, I'm not going to sweat it. Life's too short.

21 The 3 Keys to a Successful Personal History Business

A successful personal history business is like a three-legged stool. Take away one leg and you fall on your butt.

So what are the three legs? Simply put, they're passion, perseverance, and planning—or the 3P's, as I like to call them.

1. Passion

Merriam-Webster defines passion as *a strong liking or desire for or devotion to some activity, object, or concept.*

You've got to have a strong desire to tell people's stories. It's what makes you want to get up in the morning and get to work. It's what gives you that extra boost to push you through the hard times. And believe me, there will be hard times.

Without passion you'll find your work becomes a chore. Your lack of enthusiasm will inevitably lead to fewer and fewer clients finding their way to your door.

Passion is the juice that keeps you going.

2. Perseverance

Perseverance is that ability to keep going in spite of setback and difficulties. It gives your passion its backbone.

Research from the U.S. Bureau of Labor Statistics suggests, "most failures of American startups will occur in the first two years of their existence."

If you're expecting to turn a profit within a year, you'll be sorely disappointed. It'll take at least two years or more to get your personal history business up and running.

Without perseverance it's all too easy to give up when the going gets tough.

3. Planning

> *Planning is an unnatural process; it is much more fun to do something. The nicest thing about not planning is that failure comes as a complete surprise, rather than being preceded by a period of worry and depression.* —Sir John Harvey-Jones

There's wisdom in Sir John's tongue-in-cheek put-down. It's true that doing something is much more fun than planning. That's why I suspect many small business owners don't have a business plan.

But if you don't have a business plan, it doesn't matter how much passion and perseverance you have. You're rudderless and you'll almost certainly run aground.

I'm not suggesting you have to take a year to write a 40-page monster plan. What you need is something that's relatively simple. According to *WiseBread* your plan should address such questions as:

- What's my product or service?
- Who are my clients?
- How will I reach my clients?
- What are my goals over the next 3, 6, and 12 month period?
- What are my fixed, variable, and capital expenses?
- How much do I have to charge to make a profit?

For more help on planning check out these resources:

- *Making Business Plans Easy* (http://smallbiz-trends.com/2010/04/making-business-plans-easy.html)
- *The One Page Business Plan for the Creative Entrepreneur* (http://www.onepagebusinessplan.com/)
- *How to Write a Business Plan* (http://articles.bplans.com/writing-a-business-plan/)

Conclusion

I see newcomers who go into the personal history business, full of passion for helping people tell their stories. This is good but it's not enough. It's just one leg on our three-legged stool. Sadly, without the other legs of perseverance and planning, some of these same people give up their dream.

22 10 Commandments for the Professional Personal Historian

I'm not Moses or even a prophet for that matter. But I've been around for a while! I've learned some key lessons that can be summed up in these ten commandments that I try my best to follow. Not always successfully!

For those of you starting out, these might provide a useful checklist. For the experienced among us, perhaps the commandments will be a useful reminder of what we need to keep doing.

1. Create a dedicated home office space.

If you can spare a room with a door that closes, all the better. You want to create a space that says, "This is where I work. Do not disturb." The added value is that at the end of the day you can close the door and leave your work behind.

2. Learn to say NO.

You'll find this is a crucial commandment. You want to be able to say *No* to a client that wants you to work for less than you're worth. You want to be able to say *No* to taking on a client you don't like. You need to say *No* to taking on more work than you can handle.

3. Take time off.

I know that when you're self-employed, it's easy to work every day. But this is a recipe for burnout. While there'll be times when deadlines loom, make certain to find some down time during the day and the week. Schedule these times in your calendar. If you don't, chances are you'll just keep on working.

4. Schedule a part of each week for marketing.

For most of us the idea of marketing is about as much fun as going to the dentist. And like the dentist, if we don't schedule regular marketing activities, we'll be in trouble down the road. The important thing is to build marketing into your weekly schedule, whether it's an hour a day or once a week. Make a date and stick to it.

5. Join a professional association.

I'm a member of the *Association of Personal Historians* and it has been a great source of support and training. Through an association like APH you can develop your skills, meet some great people, and improve your professional credibility with your clients.

6. Have a mentor.

Working on your own can be lonely. You need to find someone in your community that you can go to for support. It doesn't have to be another personal historian. It could be someone who knows how to market a home-based business. Or maybe it's another freelancer who's been in business long enough to share some insights and advice.

7. Keep educating yourself.

I find that running your own business requires many different hats. While I'm experienced at some things like video shooting and editing, I still want to know more about marketing. So I've taken workshops, read books, and subscribed to marketing newsletters. I find too that it's imperative to keep up with changing technologies.

8. Keep regular "office" hours.

Working from home can present a minefield of distractions that will eat away at your time. That's why it helps to set regular work hours that fit your particular needs. It doesn't have to be 9 to 5 but it does have to have a set start and finish time. Make sure to build into your schedule time for breaks and domestic duties.

9. Meet deadlines and deliver quality work.

Much of our success as personal historians depends on referrals from happy clients. Failing to keep to an agreed-upon delivery date or producing less than professional looking work will damage your reputation.

10. Have fun.

For me, this is absolutely critical. Being creative has a lot to do with playfulness. If you're not having fun, your work will show it. Your clients will sense your lethargy and rightly question why you're continuing to work as a personal historian.

23 The Best Advice Ever for a Personal Historian

If I were able to go back to when I began as a personal historian, what's the best advice I could give myself? Here's what I'd say.

Talk to some experienced personal historians.

Ask them about the rewards and challenges of their work. You'll get a wealth of good advice and information.

Have some cash reserves.

Plan to have six months to a year of money to live on. It's going to be financially tight as you start up. You don't need the anxiety of wondering where your next meal is going to come from.

Join the Association of Personal Historians.

This is a great group for receiving moral support as well as concrete business and creative help.

Create a business plan.

It doesn't have to be elaborate. Check out *The One Page Business Plan* (www.onepagebusinessplan.com).

Have a marketing plan.
There's lots of help out there. You might want to take a look at *A One Page Marketing Plan Anyone Can Use* (http://smallbiz-trends.com/2008/06/one-page-marketing-plan.html).

Ask yourself how well you work alone.
If you've come from a job where you worked with others, the adjustment to working alone can be a challenge. Check out my previous article *12 Key Tips for Working Successfully Alone* (15).

Remember you're a professional.
Don't give away your services. Calculate what you need to earn a year less your business expenses. This will give you a clue as to the fees you need to charge. Don't haggle with clients. It's not professional. Check out my other articles: *How Much Should You Pay a Personal Historian?* (70) and *Are You Charging Hamburger Prices for Gourmet Work?* (75).

Always have a written legal contract.
Nothing can spell disaster faster than going into a project without a contract.

Ensure your clients pay a portion of the project costs upfront.
I always have clients make an initial payment on signing the contract. This is a non-refundable deposit and provides some compensation for my time should clients back out of the project before we start. In addition, the contract stipulates a payment at the beginning of each stage of the work.

Have a financial/accounting system in place.
You need to keep a detailed record of revenue and expenses for both calculating taxes and assessing your progress. There are several good accounting programs such as *QuickBooks* that I use or *Simply Accounting*.

Perseverance.
You won't achieve success overnight. You need to plan for at least two years of slogging in order to establish your business.

Discipline.
You need to have a solid work routine and stick with it. Spending an afternoon watching daytime TV or puttering in the garden is OK now and then but don't make it a habit.

Don't waste money on print advertising.
You can't compete with the big boys and girls. Personal history clients want to be able to trust the person who is going to be recording the details of their lives. It's better to put yourself in front of potential clients through talks and workshops. In time referrals will count for a good chunk of your business.

Have a life.
Make sure that you build in down time. It's easy with your own business to work 24/7. This is a recipe for burnout and failure. Check out *Are You Part of "The Great Vacationless Class?"* (89)

24   7 Indispensable Sites for the Personal Historian

I realize that in the course of my work as a personal historian I use a variety of sites which have become indispensable to me. I'm not saying these are the only sites—you may have favorites of your own—but they're the ones I keep coming back to. Here in no particular order are my favorites:

- *iStockphoto (www.istockphoto.com):* I use this site when I'm looking for a very special, high quality, royalty-free photo. Their rates are very reasonable and the site is easy to use. It's the internet's original member-generated image and design community. You can search over four million photographs, vector illustrations, video footage, audio tracks and Flash files.
- *flickr (www.flickr.com):* A treasure trove of photos supplied by members. It's my main source of great pics to illustrate my blog posts. And what's even better—they're free!
- *Wikipedia (www.wikipedia.org):* You can find just about anything here. Wikipedia describes itself as, "written collaboratively by volunteers from all around the world; anyone can edit it. Since its creation in 2001, Wikipedia has grown rapidly into one of the largest reference web sites, attracting at least 684 million visitors yearly by 2008. There are more than 75,000 active contributors working on more than 10,000,000 articles in more than 260 languages."

- *BrainyQuote (www.brainyquote.com):* I love quotations. There are numerous sites but this one is one of my favorites. They include authors you won't find on other quotation sites.
- *OneLook Dictionary (www.onelook.com):* Currently more than 13 million words are indexed in over 1000 online dictionaries. You can find, define, and translate words all on one site.
- *JacquieLawson.com:* These are the classiest e-cards you're ever likely to find. They're all carefully hand painted and animated. I find the cards are an invaluable way to send a quick greeting to my clients. There is a modest yearly fee but you get to send as many cards as you wish.
- *CutePDF (www.cutepdf.com):* I use the free version of CutePDF whenever I need to create a PDF. Works like a charm.

25 12 Ways to Ensure Your Personal History Business Fails

[A tip of the hat to Laura Spencer at *Freelance Folder* for inspiring this chapter.]

Ever get a "teensy" bit tired of all those gung-ho blogs dedicated to productivity and success? It's time for some balance. Let's talk about good old-fashioned failure. For all you personal historians who are run off your feet with clients' demands, here's your escape plan.

Follow these 12 tips and you can't help but fail successfully.

1. Don't listen to clients.

This is perhaps the most important step. You're the one with experience, not your clients. Forget what they think they want. You know best. The sooner you turn a deaf ear to their wishes, the quicker you can lose them and fail.

2. Keep clients waiting.

You don't want to look too eager. Leave that e-mail reply and return telephone call until you feel in the mood. It's less stressful and gives the impression you're too busy to get back to them. Remember the longer you wait, the better the chance of failure.

3. Stop marketing.

It's not fun anyway. If people don't know about you, then you won't be bothered by pesky clients. Failure is guaranteed.

4. Enroll in courses, workshops, and seminars.

The trick here is to load up your plate with as many educational opportunities as you can squeeze into a day. This not only makes you terribly busy, it also leaves absolutely no time for clients.

5. Rate yourself with other more successful business owners.

Nothing can make you feel more depressed than comparing your own efforts with successful entrepreneurs. The more despondent about your own business, the quicker you can give up.

6. Watch daytime television.

Who says there's nothing on daytime TV? It's jam-packed with entertaining shows. Better yet, find a few programs with an educational bent. You know, the ones about home makeovers and cooking. That way you can convince yourself that you're gaining valuable knowledge while glued to the set for hours on end.

7. Fake competence.

Assure clients that you're capable of delivering on any type of personal history format their heart desires. Never produced a video biography? No problem. Never created a book? Piece of cake. The results will inevitably disappoint your client and ensure that bad word of mouth will drive others away.

8. Fail to meet deadlines.

People are much too obsessed with deadlines. Not to worry. You'll deliver when you can. No need to add stress to your life. As a bonus client killer, don't bother returning their calls. They probably just want to find out when their project will be delivered.

9. Spend your day on Facebook and Twitter.

It's so important to keep abreast of your friends' activities and let them know your latest news. Working on your client's project really eats into important social networking time.

10. Attend to household chores.

Working from home allows you to see what needs to be done. Your office calls out for a major cleanup. The kitchen could use a new paint job. Put your client's work on hold. After all, your needs are just as important as theirs.

11. Over promise and under deliver.
Clients can be far too picky. When you told clients they could include as many photographs as they wanted in their book, you didn't literally mean that. Really, it just takes too much time to scan all those images. Select a sample of ten photos. This is sure to disappoint your client. Bingo! Someone else who'll help drive people away from your services.

12. Don't ask for referrals.
Why do you want more clients? You need time to work on your hobbies and household chores. There's no room for more clients. Besides, asking for referrals just seems so needy.

26 10 Common Mistakes to Avoid When Starting a Personal History Business

When I launched my first business venture as a documentary filmmaker many years ago, I wish I knew then what I know now. It would have saved me a lot of grief. I'm older and "somewhat" wiser now and hope that these lessons learned from the trenches will be of help to you.

Here are 10 mistakes to avoid:

1. No savings.
Don't do what I did. I catapulted myself into the world of independent documentary filmmaking without a dime in the bank. It was gutsy but

unwise. I spent several years, desperate and struggling. Getting a personal history business up and running is going to take at least a year or two of hard effort. Give yourself some peace of mind by knowing that your savings cover those lean years. You'll sleep better at night.

2. Not charging what you're worth.

Lowering your rates in the hopes of landing a contract is a recipe for failure. Once you've set low rates, it's hard to increase them. You'll end up not making enough income to support yourself. Overworked and burned out, you'll eventually give up. Remember you're a professional with years of experience. Being underpaid does nothing for your self-esteem and nothing for your business.

3. Choosing the wrong business partner.

This is another mistake I made. I spent too much of my emotional energy resenting the fact that my partner wasn't carrying a fair share of the business load. After a year I got out of the partnership and never looked back. Don't get me wrong—a business partner can be a great asset—but choose wisely. Look for someone who shares your values and can assist you in areas where you're deficient.

4. No contract.

You don't have to produce a "door stopper" legal document. But minimally you need a letter of agreement to avoid complications. The agreement includes a project description, fees, timelines, and terms of payment.

5. Failing to say "no."

When you're starting out, it's tough to say "no" to a low paying job or to say "no" to a troublesome client. You reason that working for something is better than nothing. But time spent laboring for peanuts means missed opportunities to land some major contracts. And just because you're starting out, doesn't mean you have to suffer the "client from hell."

6. Doing everything.

I'll admit I still tend to try and do everything. And part of that is okay. What I like about being a personal historian is that I get to wear different hats. But doing everything becomes counterproductive when you take on tasks for which you have little skill. For example, I'm not adept at bookkeeping, which is why I have an accountant. And while I love graphic design and have a reasonably good eye, I would always hire a designer for a major book project.

Play to your strengths and hire out to manage your shortcomings.

7. Failing to keep detailed records.

Throwing receipts into a shoebox and then hauling them out at tax time is no way to run a business. I've done that! You need to keep an electronic record of your income and expenses on a monthly basis. This not only gives you a means of assessing the health of your enterprise but also provides accurate records for your tax return.

8. Not putting money aside for taxes.

I know from experience this can be tough. If you're barely able to pay your bills, setting aside money for the taxman seems like a non-starter.

But getting to the end of the year and finding you have a tax bill of several thousand dollars and not a penny to spare is devastating. It can lead to bankruptcy or giving up your dream to take a job to pay your taxes.

9. Failure to devote enough time to marketing.

Most personal historians I know would rather be cast off on an ice floe than market their business. Including me. But the truth is that unless people know you exist, they won't be able to hire you. And your business will fail.

The startup for any business requires extra marketing effort. This means more than putting up a web site, printing business cards, and sending out a press release. The trick is to get out of your office and go where your clients are likely to be found.

10. Pretending to be something you're not.

When you're starting out, it's natural to feel vulnerable. You worry that people won't take you seriously if they know you're a one-person operation. So there's a temptation to create a "corporate" identity that projects an image of "we" rather than "I." But honesty is the best policy. It builds trust. In today's world of box stores and indifferent mega corporations, your strength is the personal, caring attention you bring to your clients. Be proud to be a solopreneur!

Also, don't pretend you're multi-talented if you're not. If your cash flow is drying up, it's tempting to take on a lucrative project even though you've little or no expertise to pull it off successfully. You'll end up with disappointed clients and bruised self-esteem.

Conclusion

Avoiding these mistakes won't guarantee success. But they'll make your start-up more enjoyable and less likely to fail.

27 What Makes a Personal Historian a Professional?

I call myself a professional personal historian because I consider what I do and how I do it to be professional. But what does that actually mean? And who really cares?

Those of us who make our living at this business should care. Increasingly, as the recording of personal histories becomes more commonplace, our clients are going to want to know about our credentials and track record. They're going to expect professionalism. And given that our profession is still unregulated, it's up to each of us to ensure that our work meets professional standards. So what are the criteria for being a professional personal historian?

Here's my checklist.

- Belonging to an association of peers such as the Association of Personal Historians that encourages and fosters professionalism and ethical standards.
- Abiding by your association's code of ethics.
- Actively contributing to the ongoing development of the profession.

- Having a body of work that demonstrates your skill and ability to deliver a personal history project.
- Setting fees that are not consistently below the "going" rate. There isn't an established fee structure but it's possible to acquire a good sense of what personal historians are charging.
- Working full time as a personal historian.
- Seeking opportunities for further professional development.
- Requiring clients to sign written contracts and agreements for your services.

28 What You Need to Know About Becoming a Professional Personal Historian

I've been a professional personal historian now for seven years. People looking for a new direction in their professional lives occasionally ask me if they should consider becoming a personal historian.

I usually extol the virtues and tell them how much I love my work. But I've never actually thought seriously about what someone needs to consider before taking the plunge.

So if you've been thinking maybe this is the line of work for you, here's something to consider. If you can answer yes to each of the following questions, then I think you're ready.

Are you prepared to work for a year or two with little or no income?

Like any new business, it takes time to market and promote your services. So for the first couple of years you'll likely see more money going out than coming in.

Do you know what products/services you'll offer?

Personal historians offer a wide range of services and products that include ethical wills, corporate histories, editing, bookbinding, family histories, photo restoration—just to mention a few. You need to know what strengths you bring to the work.

Are you able to work alone for long periods of time?

Being self-employed can mean working days without seeing another person. If you come from a job that involves daily contact with work colleagues, you may find it difficult to adjust to the isolation.

Are you disciplined and self-motivated?

There's no boss telling you what to do. You're it! If you don't keep your office organized, prepare marketing plans and materials, and check on possible leads, no one will.

Do you have samples of your work?

Prospective clients like to be able to see the quality of your work.

Do you enjoy working with people?

For the most part personal historians work closely with their clients. If you're not a people person, then this isn't the work for you.

Do you have a support group of friends or professional colleagues?

As I mentioned earlier, being on your own can feel daunting at times. It's really important to have a group of people you can call on for professional advice and emotional support.

How did you do? Don't give up if you answered no to some of these questions. It might mean you'll have to do a little more work and planning to ensure you're ready to become a personal historian. Or the questions may have helped you see that this is not the work for you.

29 What Betty White Can Teach You About Your Personal History Business

Who doesn't love Betty White? I'm a huge fan, first encountering her as the sugar-coated tough cookie Sue Ann Nivens on *The Mary Tyler Moore Show*. Recently, I read an interview with White.

I was struck by the fact that her life has lessons to teach those of us who run personal history businesses. I'm not for a moment suggesting that we can all possess the good health and talent of a Betty White but we can certainly learn from her example.

Keep going.

Betty White has been working hard for over six decades. She's done it all, constantly reinventing herself. She started out in radio in the 1940s. Her first television appearance was in 1949 with Al Jarvis on *Hollywood on Television,* which she later hosted.

Through the '50s she created, co-produced, and starred in the syndicated comedy *Life With Elizabeth* for which she received her first Emmy Award. Through the '60s and early '70s she appeared regularly as a celebrity panelist on game shows.

Her big break came in 1973 with *The Mary Tyler Moore Show* where she was a regular until the series ended in 1977. Her next starring role, for which she received her second Emmy Award, was on *The Golden Girls* from 1985 through 1992.

Through the '90s, White guest-starred in numerous network television programs. She also lent her voice to a number of animated shows. Most recently she's hosted *Saturday Night Live* and is starring in the comedy series *Hot in Cleveland.*

- *Lesson:* Success doesn't happen overnight. As a personal historian you'll need to put in many years of hard work. You might have to take on a second job to pay the bills. Like Betty, who continually reinvented herself, you'll need to learn new skills such as public speaking, book production, blogging, or workshop design. Doing all this with determination and a positive attitude will help you through the tough times just as it did Betty White.

Celebrate your uniqueness.

Betty White embraces her age. She makes no apologies for being old. From the *Golden Girls* to *Hot in Cleveland* she's demonstrated that you can be old and still be funny, smart, outspoken, and sexy.

Receiving a lifetime-achievement award at the 2010 Screen Actors Guild Awards, she gushed sincerely about how lucky she's been to work with so many in the room, and then seamlessly added, "And I may have had some of you, too." Back on that podium again in 2011, she stroked the statuette's bare bottom and smiled lewdly.—from the Globe and Mail article "The Betty White Tornado."

- *Lesson:* Be yourself. As a personal historian, I bring decades of experience as a documentary filmmaker. I value my graying beard and wrinkles. I see my "advancing years" as a plus in this business. Age suggests experience and a life lived—valuable and marketable traits for a personal historian. Look hard at what makes you special and unique. This will be a selling point with your potential clients who are looking for authenticity as well as competency.

Embrace curiosity and learning.

"You have to stay interested in things," White said in her *Globe and Mail* interview. "There's so many things I want to know more about that I'll never live long enough to do. But it's something to reach for."

Betty White is a marvelous example of life-long learning. Starting in radio, moving to television, then becoming a producer, starring in feature films, hitting the quiz show circuit, and now releasing her fifth book *If You Ask Me: (And of Course You Won't)*.

Given her six decades in the entertainment business she could have easily succumbed to its changing technologies and tastes as many did. But she rose to the challenges, got even better, and survived without any bitterness. As she says, "Sickeningly optimistic."

- *Lesson:* To survive in the personal history business we need to adapt or be swept aside by the digital revolution. E-books, print on demand, social media, and HD video all require learning new ways of doing our work. Sure, it's not easy at times but sticking our heads in the sand or complaining bitterly won't work. Grab on to your inner "Betty White" and just do it!

Look fantastic.

Have you noticed that throughout her career Betty White always looks fabulous and stylish? She's not afraid to show some flair and sassiness.

Lesson: Hire a designer to ensure that all of your marketing materials—business cards, brochures, and website are first class. Don't be afraid to step out of your comfort zone to come up with a design that speaks to your uniqueness. And don't forget your own appearance. Looks do speak volumes whether we like it or not. You want your business attire to read confident, impeccable, trustworthy, and appropriate.

30 8 Ways to Make Your Business Stand Out From the Crowd

In today's marketplace you've got to do more than offer excellent service and product. That's a given. To separate your small business from all the others offering a similar service you've got to be unique and memorable. How do you do that?

Begin by checking out your competition. Look at their websites, blogs, and any printed marketing material. Ask yourself, "What can I do that they're not doing?"

Taking my own advice, I started doing a little research on a few personal history websites. Here's what I learned.

Generally personal historians do a good job of extolling the virtues of recording life stories. But there are omissions. This means there's a real opportunity for you to fill the gaps and set your personal history business apart. Here are 8 ways to be unique:

1. Provide a money-back guarantee.

This provides real comfort for potential clients. It also says that you're confident about the quality of your work. I had a 100% satisfaction-guaranteed label on my home page and it was never a problem.

2. Contribute to your community.

Demonstrate your values by listing your volunteer activities. Consider donating a percentage of your profits to a charity that has an obvious connection to life stories such as the *Alzheimer's Association* or *Reading is Fundamental*.

3. Have a toll free number.

Prominently display your toll free number on your home page and other marketing materials. The easier it is for potential clients to talk to you, the better the chance of securing that client.

4. Offer free resources.

Put together a series of lists and mini-publications like *15 Great Memoirs Written by Women, The 50 Best Life Story Questions,* and *Come to Your Senses and Unlock Childhood Memories* (these resources are available in my other book for personal historians, *Skills for Personal Historians: 102 Savvy Ideas to Boost Your Expertise*).

5. List prices.

There's no getting away from it, price matters. It's usually the first thing people want to know. Anything that hints at avoidance can lead to suspicion. I know that personal history fees vary widely depending on the scope of a project. But minimally you can indicate a range. For example: Prices range from $300 for a one-hour video interview to $10,000 for a documentary film biography.

6. Go green.

Consumers increasingly expect businesses to limit their environmental impact. Being green can set you apart. How do you reduce your carbon footprint? In your office do you use recycled paper, compact fluorescent bulbs or LED lights? Do you drive a fuel-efficient car? Does an environmentally responsible company do your printing?

Consider buying carbon offsets. In Canada, one of the top ranked companies is *Less*. In the United States check out *TerraPass*. Make sure that your clients know your commitment to the environment is more than talk.

7. Be an expert.

Write articles that offer tips and advice. These can be on your own blog or for sites such as *EZineArticles.com* and *About.com*. In time you'll be seen as an expert!

8. Follow a Code of Ethics.

If you're a member of the Association of Personal Historians (if you're not, you should be), you know that you're expected to adhere to the APH Code of Ethics. It's simple to add this as a page to your website. Like the money back guarantee it creates a degree of comfort for your clients.

Conclusion.

If I were a potential client in search of a personal historian, who would I hire?

Over and above the obvious need to hire a personal historian with a high degree of expertise, the nod would go to the person who was not only outstanding but went that extra mile and met the above attributes.

31 Do You Want To Be a Successful Personal Historian?

Why do some succeed and others fail? In a word, *persistence*. It's that ability to get knocked down, pick yourself up, and keep going. Success of course is entirely in the mind of the beholder. Success to one person is failure to another.

Increasingly people find their way to my blog looking for the key to a successful career as a personal historian. I don't have a magic formula. But what I do know from years of experience is that without persistence nothing of real value can be achieved.

There are plenty of obstacles on the road to becoming a successful personal historian. I've selected four. Your success will largely be determined by whether you persist and overcome these obstacles.

The Isolation Obstacle

Your home office can be a lonely place. This is especially true if you previously worked in a business where you socialized with fellow employees.

There are ways to minimize the isolation. You can network through social media, join professional associations, and participate in service organizations. But the truth is that a good part of your personal history work will be accomplished alone.

Failure to overcome this isolation can give you second thoughts about being a personal historian.

The Fear Obstacle

This is the biggest obstacle to your success.

There's so much to fear when starting a new personal history business. There's the fear of marketing yourself, the fear of doing the wrong thing, the fear of not having enough money to live on, the fear of being an incompetent interviewer, and on and on.

Fear can paralyze. An ability to keep going in spite of your fears spells the difference between success and failure.

The Cash Flow Obstacle

If you're used to a regular paycheck, get ready for a shock. For the first couple of years you'll find more money going out than coming in.

In order to persist through the lean times you'll need to be able to call on all your financial ingenuity. If you don't have a reserve of funds, or a part-time income or the support of friends and family or the thriftiness of a Scotsman, you may not be able to continue.

The Experience Obstacle

Personal historians come from a wide range of professions but no one comes to the business fully experienced. It's the kind of work you learn over time and largely by doing.

There are a host of basic skills you need—marketing, interviewing, editing, project management, and sales, to mention a few. Being able to clearly identify your business shortcomings and showing persistence in overcoming them spells the difference between success and failure.

Conclusion

Let me leave you with these inspiring words on persistence by American naturalist and author, Edward O. Wilson.

> *"You are capable of more than you know. Choose a goal that seems right for you and strive to be the best, however hard the path. Aim high. Behave honorably. Prepare to be alone at*

times, and to endure failure. Persist! The world needs all you can give."

32 How to be Self-Employed and Stay Motivated

When we are motivated by goals that have deep meaning, by dreams that need completion, by pure love that needs expressing, then we truly live life. ~ Greg Anderson

Most of my working life I've been self-employed, first as a documentary filmmaker and now as a personal historian. There have been ups and downs but on the whole I've been able to stay motivated. What's the secret? Here are the things that have worked for me.

Believe in what you're doing.
This is crucial. If you're not happy with what you're working at, then it's almost impossible to stay motivated. For me, I know that being a personal historian satisfies some of my deepest values. It's something I wrote about in *Why Are You a Personal Historian?*, one of the ideas I shared in my other book for personal historians, *Skills for Personal Historians*.

Take a break from your work.
No matter how passionate you are about your work, your motivation will wane if you don't take time off. Now it doesn't have to be a month in Tahiti although that does sound enticing. I'm talking about something simpler—things like getting away from your computer for 15 to 20

minute breaks every hour or two, making sure to take a day for yourself at least once a week, and planning a major holiday every year.

Ensure you have an attractive place to work.

If your heart sinks every time you head to your work place, something's wrong. Take a hard look at your office. Is it dark and cluttered with ugly mismatched furniture? You'll be more motivated if your office is a place where you actually like to work. Make sure it has some natural light, ergonomic furniture, your favorite colors, and some attractive pictures on the wall. I love my office, which occupies the front of the second floor of our house. It has two large windows that face east and look out on a small park across the street.

Remind yourself of the benefits.

I only worked as a salaried employee for a fraction of my work life but I know what I didn't like about it. There were the office politics, incompetent managers, endless, often nonproductive meetings, and commuting, to name but a few. Being self-employed I have the benefits of setting my own goals and pace. I can select the kind of projects I want to do. I decide the fees to charge and when to take a break. Reminding myself of these benefits is a great motivator.

Have your very own cheerleaders.

If you work on your own, it can be isolating. You need to have people who'll be there to sympathize with you, give you a boost, and offer timely advice. The Association of Personal Historians is another source of support. This is a group of colleagues who understand what I'm going through and provide great advice 24/7.

Create variety.

No matter how much you love your work, it can become a bore and a drain on your motivation if you're always doing the same thing. That's why I like to challenge myself to find different or better ways to deliver my personal history services. I started with video life stories and then tried my hand at books. Now I have this blog. I find I'm stretched and stimulated and continually motivated.

33 When Should You Quit Being a Personal Historian and Move On?

Some of you may be wondering if it's time to give up being a personal historian all together. Remember there's nothing wrong with quitting. I write about giving up in *Stop With The Productivity Pitches!* (87).

I've changed careers at least four times in my life. From my experience here are the clues that tell you enough is enough.

Lack of passion

This is a big one. To establish and run a successful personal history business requires an ongoing belief that what you're doing is vital. You must absolutely love your work. If you find that the passion has gone and your days are a grind, then it's time to move on.

Lack of income

We all need to make enough money to pay the bills and have a little extra left over. For everyone that amount will vary. But if you've been working hard for a couple of years and you're still having trouble making ends meet, you might want to reconsider being a personal historian. Nothing can kill your passion quicker than a dwindling bank account.

Lack of energy

Keeping a business flourishing requires energy. There are ongoing marketing, networking, client projects, and administrative tasks. If you find that you don't have the energy because of poor health, age, or caregiving responsibilities, you might want to call it quits.

Lack of time

A successful personal history business is a full-time job. If you're trying to run it while juggling other part-time jobs, you could face a crisis. While you may need extra income to keep yourself afloat, it makes it difficult to grow your personal history business. If you're in this situation, consider giving it up and making personal history a hobby—not a business.

Conclusion

Quitting is okay. I would caution though not to quit too early. Collective wisdom says that it takes at least two years to get a new business up and running. So give it time.

Some of the challenges I've mentioned above might be overcome by altering your approach. For example, a lack of passion may be a result of exhaustion rather than a lack of interest. Finding a way to bring some balance into your life might bring back the passion.

Before making your final decision to move on, weigh all the factors, look for possible solutions, and talk with trusted colleagues and friends. If it still looks like quitting is the answer, go for it!

34 Would You Hire Yourself?

Every time we meet potential clients, we have to prove ourselves. They're sizing us up and assessing whether we're the right fit for them. Here's a cheeky question. Would you hire yourself? My quick reply is of course I'd hire myself. Why wouldn't I? Here's a list of my qualities and skills:

Strengths

- Friendly
- A calm and inquisitive nature
- Good listener
- Reliable
- Sense of humor
- Meets deadlines
- Six years in business and a proven track record
- Testimonials and references from previous clients
- Prior life and work experience that shows a connection to my current interest in personal histories
- Membership in two professional associations: the Association of Personal Historians and the Canadian Hospice Palliative Care Association.

Weaknesses

This sounds like a pretty good list. Right? But here's the catch. What's missing? Some years ago I did a little self-examination that revealed some cracks in this otherwise "sterling" picture of myself. And to be honest, these weaknesses contributed to the loss of potential clients. Here's what my analysis revealed:

- I was focusing more on "selling" rather than "soliciting the needs" of the client.
- I failed to show samples of my work.
- I wasn't precise and clear about my pricing.
- I didn't offer alternative personal history products that clients might find more within their price range.
- I failed to show my passion for recording life stories.

I've since worked on these weak points and can now claim that I'm almost perfect! But seriously, we all need to do a periodic self-examination and ask, "Would I hire myself?" You might be surprised at what you find.

Self-assessment

It's your turn to shine a light on your abilities and shortcomings as a personal historian. Here are some questions to get you started:

- Have you a body of work you're prepared to show potential clients?
- Do you get projects delivered on time?
- Are you clear about your fees and how they're structured?
- Do you have a "stick with it" attitude or give up easily?

- What have you done in the past six months to keep up with changing technologies?
- Do you belong to any professional associations? How active are you in them?
- Do you present yourself in a professional manner?
- Are you a good listener and able to empathize with people?
- How much experience do you have in running your own business?
- Do you have testimonials available for distribution?
- Do you offer a variety of products and services?
- How do you show passion for your work?

CHAPTER 3:
Getting & Keeping Clients

35 #1 Secret to Getting More Clients

You're talented and motivated. You've got business cards, a website, and brochures. But you've few clients. So here's the #1 secret to getting more clients. *Get noticed!*

That's right. Clients need to know you exist. Here are 10 ways to get noticed:

Join a community group.
Find a group of people who share your interests. Members will naturally begin to inquire about your work. In time you'll get client leads.

Give talks.
Develop a 10 to 15 minute presentation not about you but on a topic related to your work. Contact service clubs and offer to make a presentation.

Run workshops.
Put together a workshop on how to do something. Make it practical and have useful handouts with your contact information clearly visible.

Send out media releases.
Take advantage of special holidays to send out a media release that ties the holiday in with the service you provide.

Create a blog.
Setting up a blog is simple with free blogging platforms like Blogger, Typepad, and WordPress. Write frequent, useful, fresh, and entertaining articles aimed at your target clients.

Join local business and professional groups.
Every community has opportunities for networking. Go to mixers and meet people.

Write articles.
Nothing helps enhance your credibility and visibility than an article in a magazine, newspaper, or newsletter.

Host your own radio program.
With Blog Talk Radio (www.blogtalkradio.com) you can create your own online radio show.

Publish an online newsletter.

Newsletters establish you as an authority and allow you to keep in touch with your audience.

Join Toastmasters.

This is not only a great way to practice and improve your public speaking abilities but also a way to find clients and get referrals.

36 3 Keys to Creating Trust with Potential Clients

Here's a shocker! I was reading that a CBS News/New York Times Poll revealed *only 30 percent of respondents believed people in general are trustworthy.* Not surprising perhaps but disillusioning.

But all's not lost. When a similar group was asked, "What percent of people *that you know* are trustworthy?" the response jumped to 70 percent. Clearly, knowing someone makes a big difference. The more people get to know us, the higher the level of trust. It makes sense.

A key factor in whether potential clients will hire us as personal historians is trust. But how do you build trust in an introductory meeting?

I turned to the *Oxford Dictionary* for help. It defines trust as *a firm belief in the reliability, truth, or ability of someone or something.* If we take each of these components of trust, they provide clues to building rapport with a new client.

Reliability.

Reliability begins with the simplest of acts—showing up on time for your meeting. Nothing kills reliability more than changing an already fixed appointment date or showing up late or early.

It also helps if you've been in business for a few years, have a track record, and have a set of glowing testimonials.

Avoid being needy. It reeks of desperation and raises questions about the health of your business. No one wants to sign a contract with someone who is about to go under.

Truth.

Refrain from being somebody you're not. People can smell phoniness. You don't have to adopt a "marketing" persona or be over solicitous. Go into your meeting with a new client with confidence, friendliness, and mindfulness. That's it, nothing more.

Forgo trying to be all things to all people. For example, if your specialty is producing video biographies, don't "fudge" things by selling yourself as a book specialist in hopes of getting the job. You won't sound convincing. It's better to recommend a colleague whose expertise is print. You'll win points for being honest. While you might lose the contract, your good name will spread in the community. And that matters.

We all expect straight answers. Your clients are no different. Questions about your fees, expertise, years of experience, and the time to complete a personal history need to be answered without obfuscation.

Ability.

If you're new to personal histories, you may have little to show prospective clients. But this doesn't mean that you can't highlight your previous experience to establish your proficiency. For example, print and video editing, interviewing, counseling, radio and film producing all require skills that come to play in producing a print or video life story.

You want to display your interviewing expertise from the moment you meet your prospective client. If you're friendly, curious, attentive, and non-judgmental, then you'll have modeled good interviewing skills. This is subtle "selling" but it works in establishing trust and rapport.

37 7 Questions to Ask Before Taking on a New Personal History Client

What's worse than having no clients at all? If you said "having the client from hell," you're absolutely right. Here are seven questions to ask yourself that will ensure that you don't end up working with Satan's cousin.

Do I have the time?

Look carefully at what's on your plate right now. This should include not only current projects but also ongoing business tasks such as networking, promotion, and bookkeeping. Don't forget to factor in personal chores such as shopping, caregiving, and cleaning. No one wants to say no to potential work. But you also want to do the best for your client while at the same time not become over- extended.

Is this a client I like?

One of the pleasures of being a personal historian is that we get to work with some incredibly interesting people. If you find that your potential client exhibits behavior and expresses beliefs that are antithetical to yours, you should seriously question continuing with that client. Remember, you'll be spending many hours together and you don't want to be continually agitated by someone you basically don't like.

Am I a good fit for this client?

Each of us tends to specialize. In my case it's video life stories although I have done some books. If your potential client is looking for a life story in a format in which you haven't much experience, then consider referring that client to someone who does have the expertise. You'll gain the respect of your client for being forthright. If you still want to take on this client, do you have access to people who could help you in those areas where you're less proficient?

Does this client have the support of other family members?

Families can be messy—not at all like those Norman Rockwell paintings. You don't want inadvertently to get yourself into some long-standing family squabble. Ask if your client has discussed this undertaking with other family members. Are they supportive? Are there concerns? If there hasn't been any discussion, then have your client bring together all the parties concerned so that you can talk to the group about what's involved and answer questions.

Am I treated as a professional?

Remember you *are* a professional. If you're like me, you've had decades of experience in a field related to personal history, have a university degree or two, and have a portfolio of personal history projects. So watch out for potential clients who fail to return calls, keep changing appointment times, forget meetings, try to "nickel and dime" you to death, and imply that their "cousin Bob" could do the work for half the price. None of this is in keeping with treating you as a professional. No one would treat a lawyer, accountant, or doctor that way. You shouldn't put up with this kind of behavior either.

Is this potential client the one who will be paying me?

From my experience, it's not uncommon for the person requesting my service not to be the same person paying for it. For example, a daughter may inquire about doing a personal history for her mother but it is the parent who will be paying for the work. From the beginning it's important to establish who is paying for your service. You want to have all the principal players in the same room so that you can explain the process directly and address any concerns that may arise. Failure to do this can mean that misinterpreted information is relayed and additional meetings may be needed to clarify. This is not a productive use of time.

Will working with this client stretch me professionally?

I don't know about you, but I thrive on challenges. If I had to do the same thing day-in and day-out, I'd be bored. Now it's a truism that clients pay you for what you know, not what you need to know. It may sound as if I'm contradicting Question Three above. However, if you tell your client you'd enjoy taking on the challenge of expanding your skills, you might gain their support. You can sweeten the deal by offering your service at a lower than normal fee to compensate for your learning.

*[Thanks to **Web Worker Daily** for suggesting this topic.]*

38. Are You Showing Your Clients How Much You Appreciate Them?

You may have seen the inspiring video "Johnny the Bagger" (https://www.youtube.com/watch?v=sepARXV8MRI). It's the true story of how one young man with Down Syndrome changed the experience of grocery shoppers in a simple but profound way.

This video spoke to me powerfully. With imagination and heart we can go that extra mile to show gratitude to our clients.

Here are some suggestions for demonstrating our appreciation as personal historians.

- a framed poster of the front cover of your client's book or DVD
- birthday and holiday greetings
- a small box of heirloom family cookies along with the recipe
- a jar of your homemade preserves
- a copy of the APH Anthology *My Words Are Gonna Linger: The Art of Personal History*
- a gift certificate from a local bookstore
- a donation in your client's name to a "memory" or "literacy" related charity such as the *Alzheimer's Association* or *Reading Is Fundamental*
- a box of nostalgia note cards

What are some of the special ways you say "thank you?"

39 Are Your Clients Extremely Satisfied With Your Service?

I was in my neighborhood bank today and as I was coming out, I noticed a sign that read: *We hope your experience with us today was extremely satisfying.* I thought it a bit odd. Most of my banking is pretty perfunctory. As long as the ATM doesn't screw up, I'm pretty delighted. But the sign got me thinking. What would make your personal history service extremely satisfying for clients? Here's what I think.

Always keep appointments and show up precisely on time.

I'm a stickler about punctuality. The quickest way to make me an "unhappy camper" is to show up late. By being punctual we show respect for our client's time.

Listen carefully to what your clients want, not what you think they should have.

This goes back to a point I made in my previous article *Attention Introverts You can Market Successfully!* (55) and that is solve, don't sell.

Provide your clients with a range of options within their price range.

Clients like to see that you're not trying to sell them the deluxe package and are genuinely concerned about giving them the best for what they can afford.

Smile.
Not all the time, of course! Otherwise you'll have people dialing 911. But you know what I mean. Even if your client drives you nuts, don't let your frustration show on your face.

Don't haggle.
Remember you're a professional. Be clear about your services and fees and be accommodating. But avoid getting into a "nickel and diming" conversation. If your client can't afford your services, suggest an alternative service. And remember the point above. Keep smiling!

Make the interview experience memorable.
This means asking insightful and powerful questions that unlock the richness of a person's life.

Deliver on time.
Unless there are very good reasons for being late, delivering on or before a specified date is very satisfying.

Provide more than the client expected.
Some ideas: a framed copy of the book cover, a complimentary copy of the book or DVD, a personalized gift of homemade jam, cookies, or relish with the heirloom recipe included, or a book by their favorite author.

Keep in touch.
Send a thank you card after delivering your client's personal history. Note birthdays and special holidays and make a point of sending a card.

40 Are Your Clients Getting Too Little?

Recently I was reading an article by marketing provocateur Seth Godin. In his usual challenging manner he hit the nail on the head.

> *The hard part isn't charging a lot. The hard part is delivering more (in the eye of the recipient) than he paid for...Too often, in the race to charge less, we deliver too little. And in the race to charge more, we forget what it is that people want. They want more. And better.*

A personal history book or video is a big ticket item for most clients. So what can we do to demonstrate that our clients will get more than they expected?

Here are some ideas that come to mind:

Emphasize the lasting value of a life story.

When you have an initial conversation with a potential client, use words such as *investment* rather than *cost*, *legacy* rather than *personal history*, *gift* instead of *book* or *video*.

I sometimes use a new car analogy. I point out that as soon as you drive a car off the lot, it begins to depreciate. On the other hand, a life story appreciates over time. You can't say that about many things.

Be sure the client knows your professional qualifications. It's true that "Cousin George" can probably do the book for half the price. But does he have the experience and professional background to do a first-class job? When people hire me, they know that not only are they getting an experienced professional personal historian but also a former award-winning documentary filmmaker. My work will be better than "Cousin George's." At least I hope so. Look for ways you can make your qualifications stand out.

Give your client more than just a book.

There are a number of ways to add extras:

- Include a set of audio CDs of your interviews.
- Provide a poster size duplication of the book cover.
- Give a subscription to a family history magazine.
- Reproduce a treasured archival photo from the book and have it framed.
- Organize a launch party for friends and family after the book's publication.

Find those little extras that add more value to your work.

Emphasize the superior quality of your books.

Show one of your beautiful personal history books to the client. The quality will speak for itself. Point out the exceptional archival paper stock and inks that are used. Acquaint clients with the outstanding design elements. You want to convey the message that these are "Legacy" books that will last for generations.

Stress the good feelings that come with a personal history book or video.

What clients may not appreciate are the positive feelings that arise with personal histories. It's not just a book or video. Parents and children talk about feeling closer to each other after engaging in a life story. Parents are touched by the thoughtfulness of their children undertaking such an endeavor. Still other recipients of a personal history find a new appreciation for their life accomplishments.

A personal history is a connection to the soul.

41 Guess What? Not Everyone Wants a Life Story Told

I know. I know. This isn't news to you, right? But I think deep down we personal historians secretly believe that if we find the right combination of price, promotion, and product, people won't be able to resist us. Clients will be beating down our door. Wrong! Even if you give your services away for free, you still won't get many takers. Let me explain.

I initiated and have coordinated a life stories program at Victoria Hospice. This is a free service. It provides patients registered with Hospice an opportunity to be audio interviewed about their life by a trained Hospice volunteer. The majority of those approached decline the offer. Why? I don't know for certain but I suspect these are some of the reasons:

- Some people nearing the end of life have too many physical and emotional issues and can't cope with the notion of adding one more thing to do.
- For some, committing to a life story may feel too much like wrapping things up—like making funeral arrangements.

- For others, there's a sense that their lives haven't been significant enough to warrant a life story.
- Some are uncomfortable with the idea of talking about their lives to a stranger.
- For others, there's the feeling that to record their life story is "tooting your own horn."

Your clients may not be receiving palliative care. But when I look at my list, I realize that these obstacles apply just as well to the people you're trying to reach. If you stood on the main intersection of your hometown with a big placard that read "Free Personal Histories," do you know what? Very few would sign up.

So here's the thing. Don't beat yourself up! If you're doing what you can to market and promote your business and the telephone isn't ringing off the hook, it really may have nothing to do with you. Take a deep breath, pour yourself a drink, and forget about marketing for now. On the other hand if you're feeling masochistic, you can read some of my other articles on marketing and small business.

- *What Do Fishing and Personal History Clients Have in Common?* (57)
- *#1 Secret to Getting More Clients* (35)
- *5 Tips to Overcoming Your Marketing Blues* (50)
- *How to Go For The Gold in Your Business* (2)
- *The Introvert's 12 Step Plan for Painless Networking* (54)

42 How You Can Provide a "Ritz-Carlton" Welcome for Potential Clients

I read a news article the other day on the opening of the upscale Ritz-Carlton Hotel in Toronto. What caught my attention was the hotel's philosophy of creating a "warm and sincere greeting" so that patrons become "Ritz-Carlton guests for life." The company's own polling shows that the first ten minutes are critical. Fail to impress guests in that time frame and you've lost them.

What can we do as personal historians to create a "Ritz-Carlton" welcome for our clients? I must admit that my own approach might be charitably called the "Holiday Inn" welcome—friendly but decidedly not upscale. I think there's room for improvement.

Here are a few ideas that we could all use to make potential clients feel special:

Be on time.

Call me old-fashioned but punctuality is a professional given. Show up at your client's home on time—not 5 minutes early or 5 minutes late. Punctuality conveys a sense of trustworthiness, meticulousness, and courtesy. Don't underestimate its importance.

First impressions count.

Casual weekend attire won't do. Dress in a manner that conveys confidence, timeless style, and appropriateness. This doesn't mean dressing in a power suit. For men a pair of neatly pressed slacks, sports coat, crisp shirt, and polished dress shoes will fit the bill. I hesitate to suggest fashion advice for women other than erring on the conservative side. This means easy on the bling and use of color.

It's about them not you.

Forget about selling. No one wants to be sold anything. You're visiting a potential client to listen to their hopes, wishes, and concerns about recording a life story. You want to be asking questions that get at the heart of why the client has asked to see you—questions like: "What is important for you about preserving this story? What concerns do you have about not getting this story told? How will this project affect your life? What do you hope this personal history project will look like?"

Only when you've a clear understanding of what your client wants, can you turn the conversation to questions of approach, process, time, and costs.

Don't avoid addressing the cost question.

It will more than likely pop up early in the conversation. Explain, "Costs are variable depending on the size of the project. I really want to get a better idea of what you hope for so that I can provide you with a more precise cost estimate."

Don't overstay your welcome.

Just as arriving on time is important so too is leaving on time. If you and your client agreed on an hour, respect that. Don't go over unless your client indicates that this would be acceptable.

Leave gracefully.

No matter how the meeting turns out, your "Ritz-Carlton" approach demands a "classy" exit. There are the obvious things like expressing thanks for being invited to listen to the client and to share your knowledge about personal histories.

If you want to take that extra step that will have your client talking about you for some time, here's what you can do.

- Give a gift book that illustrates the historical development of the community in which your client lives.
- Present an attractive journal for writing down memories.
- Offer a gift book such as *My Words Are Gonna Linger: The Art of Personal History.*
- Send a thank you card that includes a $25 bookstore gift card.
- Don't be afraid to spend $20 to $30 dollars on a gift. It's part of your marketing budget. And if it helps you to land a $10,000 to $15,000 contract, it's a small price to pay.

43 How to Get Mom or Dad to Tell a Life Story

Sometimes I encounter an adult son or daughter who's had no success in convincing a parent to record a life story.

My experience has been that if people are really reluctant, it may be very hard to nudge them into documenting their lives. I hope these tips may be of help.

Don't make it sound daunting.

You don't want to create the impression that your parents have to toil away writing down every detail of their lives from birth to the present. You might say something like, "Mom, you've told me some great stories over the years. I'd really like to capture some of them so that your grandchildren will know more about your life. It would be a wonderful gift for them."

Explain that you'll help.

You can say something like, "I can bring over a recorder and we could just sit and chat about some of your favorite memories. What do you think?"

Suggest some different approaches.

There's more than one way to tell a life story. You can do it chronologically or thematically. Or you can focus on major turning points.

Counter the myth.

One of the favorite reasons for not documenting a life story is the one that goes, "Oh my life isn't all that interesting." Sound familiar? Explain to your parent that you're not looking for *interesting*. What you treasure are the stories that illuminate a different time. What you want to know is what it was like living before the advent of television, computers, supermarkets, and so on. What you value is the wisdom accumulated along the way—the life lessons. What you want to hear are the things that made mom or dad proud, happy, and sometimes sad.

44 What Do You Do When Facing a Reluctant Family Storyteller?

How many personal historians have found themselves in this situation? You have an enthusiastic client, an adult child who really wants her mom or dad's life story told, but the parent is reluctant.

Behind the reluctance are usually a host of fears. But the fears expressed are not always the ones that are causing the hesitancy. I found myself in such a situation. I made several visits and telephone calls to a daughter and mother over the course of a month. The daughter was anxious to have her mother begin a life story project but her mother wasn't.

The daughter explained that her mother was insistent on first going through her collection of photos and letters. What eventually became apparent was that the mother was in the early stages of dementia and was fearful of not being able to recall past events. Unfortunately, we never got started.

In two other articles, I wrote about such reluctance and some possible solutions:

- *Guess What? Not Everyone Wants a Life Story Told* (41)

- *How to Get Mom or Dad to Tell a Life Story* (43)

More fears, more solutions

Since writing those articles, I've expanded the list of fears that dissuade some people from being interviewed. And I've suggested some possible solutions to these fears.

I'd like to add that none of these solutions are possible without a face-to-face meeting with the subject of the personal history. People need to see and hear you before they can decide if they're comfortable enough to let you into their life.

The fear
Unpleasant and best forgotten stories will arise and cause me distress.

Possible solution
Explain to the interviewee that before starting you always ask if there are any parts of the person's life story you should avoid. Make it clear that it's perfectly acceptable for the interviewee not to answer questions that are about too sensitive a subject.

The fear
An inability to remember events, names, and dates will make me look foolish.

Possible solution
At the outset, explain that what is important are the stories not the names and dates. You might add, "For example, I could ask you if you have a childhood event that's particularly memorable? Would you have something to tell me?" I find everyone has a favorite childhood story.

Also mention that the interviews will be done chronologically. There'll be time for reflection by the interviewee and an opportunity to jot down some notes in preparation for each interview session.

The fear

I've never been interviewed before and don't know what to expect or how to act.

Possible solution

Most people's knowledge of interviewing comes from watching TV news and public affairs shows. These can be provocative, hard hitting, and sometimes sensational. No wonder people have some apprehension about being interviewed!

It's important to address that fear by pointing out that a personal history interview is more like a conversation between friends. It isn't an interrogation. Also explain that the interview is in their control. You won't ask questions they don't want asked and they are free to stop at any point if they're unhappy with the interview.

The fear

I don't have anything worthwhile to say.

Possible solution

This is a common fear. Explain that every life has stories that'll be of interest to families and future generations. We bring to the interview the wisdom of our experience. We've lived through interesting times and can talk about it from a personal perspective. We've had heartaches and successes and have lessons to share. All of this is compelling stuff.

The fear

I might say something that will unintentionally cause heartache for a family member.

Possible solution

Assure the interviewee that anything said can be edited from the interview. The person will also have an opportunity to read the final draft of the book or view a fine cut of the video. If there is still something that the interviewee doesn't feel comfortable with, it can be removed.

The fear

If I have my life story told, people will think I'm putting on airs.

Possible solution

Explain that outside of the immediate family no one need know the interviewee has published a personal history. Family members are the ones who'll be most interested in the stories and want to see the project proceed.

45 Warning: Documenting Your Life Story Could be Fatal

Not really but we're a superstitious bunch. Step on a crack, break your mother's back. The number 13, black cats and walking under a ladder—all unlucky. We can add another—writing your life story means death is imminent. It sounds absurd but from my experience this fear is alive and well.

I've had adult children of aging parents approach me and say, "We'd like to get Mom's life story recorded but we're afraid she'll think that her time is almost up." I've also had some folks in their 70s tell me, "I'm not dead yet! I'll get around to my life story later on."

So what's the basis of this reluctance? I think that none of us really wants to confront the fact that we're mortal. Of course, we know that one day the lights will go out—but not today, thank you very much and hopefully not for a long time. So when the idea of recording one's life story comes up it sounds as if we're doing a wrap up—kind of like writing your will and pre-arranging your funeral. As I said, we don't want to be reminded of our mortality.

What's the solution? You need to confront the elephant in the room. Don't skip around the question of mortality. You might say something like, "You know Mom, you're not getting any younger and sadly some day you won't be around to tell us the wonderful stories of your life. You know so much family history. I know that one day your grandchildren and their children will be so grateful that you took the time to record your stories. Right now you're in good health and able to do this. What do you think? Can we get started this week?"

If you encounter some hesitancy, ask Mom if there are questions she might have about the actual work itself. She might want to know how long it will take or whether she has to remember dates and names and so on. If you answer all her questions and you still sense some reluctance, don't push. If you push too hard she's likely to dig in her heels and you'll get nowhere. Just say something like, "You know Mom, let's leave it for now and next week I'll check in with you again. I really hope you'll say yes to this. It would be such a wonderful gift."

The time to begin a life story is now because we really don't know what tomorrow will bring.

CHAPTER 4:
Marketing & Promotion

46 The #1 Thing You Can Do to Jump Start Your Marketing

Marketing strategies assume one size fits all. We're told that we must network, build referrals, provide items of interest to the media, write newsletters, blog, give presentations, and so on.

News Flash! It doesn't matter if we know what we're supposed to do if we don't like doing it. And not tending to marketing tasks that we're told are critical can make us feel inept. This can quickly spiral into doing nothing at all.

For example, there's no point in telling me to get out to as many "meet and greet" events as my poor little body can manage. I'd rather have a root canal than walk around a room full of strangers pretending I'm thrilled to be there.

On the other hand, I know there are others of you who would prefer to schmooze than spend hours at a computer grinding out a newsletter.

Here's the trick. The #1 thing you can do to jumpstart your marketing is to make a plan that takes into account your personality.

If you're introverted, like me, put more energy into newsletters, blogs, and social media. And if you're an educator at heart, meeting potential clients through workshops and presentations can be satisfying.

If you're extroverted, design a plan that's people oriented. Networking events, professional groups, trade shows, and conferences will get you energized.

Conclusion

It's useful to broaden your range of marketing activities but first build on your strengths. It'll give you more confidence. Then bit by bit you can begin to add a few marketing tasks that you find more challenging.

Two of my articles that you might find helpful are: *The Introvert's 12 Step Plan for Painless Networking* (54) and *5 Tips to Overcoming Your Marketing Blues* (50).

47 5 Essential Marketing Approaches for a Successful Personal History Business

Not all marketing approaches are equal when it comes to your personal history business. Traditional print advertising, for example, isn't that effective. Few if any of us could sustain the major expense of an ad campaign. And we engage our clients at a very intimate level—which requires that they know, like, and trust us before buying our service.

So if not all marketing approaches work, what does?

The collective wisdom of personal historians who've built successful businesses suggests that these five approaches are essential.

Word-of-mouth

Having satisfied clients sing your praises to their network of family and friends is pure gold. A colleague of mine gets most of her clients by word-of-mouth. If you're starting out, it'll take some time before you've built enough critical mass to ensure a steady flow of clients.

This doesn't mean you can't begin the process with your very first client. If that person is really pleased with your work, don't forget to ask for referrals. Be sure to check out my tip on *Lousy at Getting Referrals? Here's Some Help* (52).

> *If you do build a great experience, customers tell each other about that. Word of mouth is very powerful.* — Jeff Bezos, founder of Amazon.com

Engage your community

Because our profession is a very personal business, potential clients want to be able to see, hear, and be inspired by us. So put yourself in the middle of groups where you're likely to meet face-to-face with potential clients. You can do this by volunteering, agreeing to sit on boards of community groups, and networking with business associations like

Business Network International. I've written more about this in *What Do Fishing and Personal History Clients Have in Common?* (57).

Public speaking

I know this can strike fear in the hearts of the bravest souls but don't pass up a great opportunity to promote personal histories. I've some help for you in *How to Get Control of Your Pre-Presentation Jitters* (60).

Remember that your presentation isn't about soliciting business but about educating people on the wonderful world of personal histories. Work up a variety of presentations that can fit a 15 or 30-minute time slot.

Next, contact groups in your community who might be interested in personal histories such as church groups, genealogical societies, book clubs, and service organizations.

Build referral partners

There are a number of businesses that serve some of the same clients as personal historians. These include life coaches, wedding planners, financial planners, and eldercare transition specialists.

Over time you can extend your reach by cultivating such referral partners. Read more about this in *You Can Do It! Get Referral Partners Today* (53).

Talk it up

Don't underestimate the value of mentioning your work whenever and wherever the opportunity arises. Don't be shy. Always carry a few business cards.

See your supermarket, bank, library, dentist office, and public transit as full of potential clients. Chat with a stranger in a line up or with a receptionist or librarian. It works. I've been asked for my card by a cashier at our local grocery store and by my dentist. You just never know where your next client will come from.

Make it happen!

> *Don't turn down the chance to go anywhere. Join clubs; do anything you can to get out there and meet people. You are your product. Advertise it.* ~ Max Markson, Australian marketing expert

48 25 No Cost or Low Cost Marketing Ideas for Your Personal History Business

You don't have to spend a fortune on marketing. These twenty-five ideas won't break the bank. But a word of caution. Don't try them all at once. You'll go crazy! Pick a couple and focus on them. See what works for you and then move on to some others.

1. *Business cards:* Don't forget to carry a few cards with you at all times. You never know when and where you'll have a conversation and someone will want your card. Ask businesses if they will display your card.
2. *Join a community group:* People will get to know you and in time you'll have some potential clients. I was part of a community choir for many years. It worked for me!

Marketing & Promotion

3. *Offer workshops:* This is a great way to introduce people to life stories and attract clients.

4. *Write articles:* Seek opportunities to write articles for your local paper, alumni magazine, professional newsletters, etc.

5. *Arrange speaking opportunities:* Service organizations such as the Rotary club and Lions club are always looking for guest speakers.

6. *Wear a button or T-shirt:* Have a T-shirt made with a phrase like "Preserving memories is an act of love." Wear your T-shirt when you go to the supermarket or mall.

7. *Join networking groups:* From Chambers of Commerce to Business Networking International there's a business group for you. Ask some local business people for suggestions.

8. *Start a Blog:* If you like to write and have something useful to offer potential clients, then this might be for you.

9. *Put a bumper sticker on your car:* A few words and your telephone number provides a mobile advertisement for your business.

10. *Carry a tote with a catchy "personal history" phrase:* This is similar to the T-shirt suggestion above but more suitable for business settings.

11. *Sign up and use Twitter, Facebook, and LinkedIn:* Social media has become a powerful marketing tool. Don't be left behind!

12. *Become a volunteer:* Find an organization for which you've some affinity. In time you'll find some clients among the people you'll meet.

13. *Give away gifts:* I frequent garage sales and pick up books that relate in some way to life stories. I insert a small label in the book that includes my business name and contact information. I give

these away at my workshops. You might also try bookmarks or pens.

14. *Host your own radio or TV show:* Local community radio and TV stations are always looking for new sources of programming.

15. *Join Toastmasters:* There's a Toastmasters group in most cities. It is a great way to improve your speaking abilities and also to find clients.

16. *Ask for referrals:* Don't forget to ask your satisfied clients for referrals.

17. *Publish an online newsletter:* This is an excellent way to keep in touch with clients and establish yourself as an authority.

18. *Speak at conferences:* This provides an opportunity to share your expertise and meet prospects.

19. *Join the Association of Personal Historians:* The Association provides great support and its membership listing is available to those looking to hire a personal historian.

20. *Create an e-mail signature:* Every e-mail you send out should include a memorable phrase, your web/blog address and contact information.

21. *Give away free reports:* On your blog or website create a useful document that visitors will want to read. This establishes you as an authority and also strengthens your bond with your audience.

22. *Form "supportive" business alliances:* Contact local businesses that have clients that might also fit your client profile. For example you could meet with people offering "Seniors Services." Suggest to them that it would be mutually beneficial to cross-promote your services.

23. *Attend workshops:* It's a way to enhance your professional skills and market your personal history business.

24. *Organize a charity fund-raising event:* You get to meet a lot of people, do something worthwhile, and create more awareness of your company.

25. *Send out media releases.* Tie your release to a holiday, special day, or issue. Follow up with a phone call to see if your release was received. Make friends with your local reporters. Eventually you'll get an interview.

49 Are You Using Storytelling to Promote Your Personal History Service?

For most of the 190,000 years that humans have been alive on this earth, they've learned their most important information, including survival skills, culture, religion, etc., through stories. The human brain, in fact, is wired specifically so that stories, and storytelling, have a much stronger emotional impact than information that's presented quantitatively or according to some other emotionless structure .~ marketing guru, Michael Bosworth

It's the right side of our brain that harbors our creativity and emotions. It's where storytelling has its impact. People are drawn to telling their personal histories by such deep seated desires as leaving a legacy, capturing fond memories, or finding meaning in their lives. They'll ultimately make a decision to engage your services based on emotional not quantitative information. If you're not making "storytelling" a part of your presentation, you're losing clients. In a BNET interview with Michael Bosworth he says,

> The emotional brain is where the 'aha' moments happen. Where the "I want that" or "I need that" feelings happen. The buyer has "gut reaction" and an image that allows them to make an emotional decision, such as the decision to trust someone or buy something. They can feel it and see it rather than quantifying.

How can you use storytelling to engage prospective clients?

Here are four tips:

1. Start with a story from your own experience.

Your story should convey the delight, poignancy, and impact that life stories can have for individuals and their families. For me, the article *When Small Can Be Profound* (found in *Skills for Personal Historians*) about a dying mother and her young child is a powerful reminder of the invaluable nature of our work.

2. Borrow a story.

If you don't have a personal story that suits your needs, then find one that does. For example, in my article *How a Prehistoric Cave Painting Came to My Rescue* (also shared in *Skills for Personal Historians*), I found symbolism that spoke to my suspicion that storytelling is part of our DNA. Another story I want to use some day is from James Loewen's book *Lies My Teacher Told Me*. He writes that in some African societies,

> *The recently departed whose time overlapped with people still here are the Sasha, the living dead. They are not wholly dead, for they live on in the memories of the living ... when the last person knowing an ancestor dies, that ancestor leaves the Sasha for the Zamani, the dead.*

One might say that the Zamani are *truly* dead for no one currently living knew them. What a powerful reason for ensuring that our loved one's stories are preserved so that they might continue to live in the hearts of those far into the future.

3. Be a good listener.

This shouldn't be difficult for personal historians. That's what we do! It's important to listen for the stories that are behind a person's interest in hiring you. Ask questions that will help draw these stories out. They might be stories that relate to leaving a recorded legacy or perhaps a document that speaks to their beliefs, values, and wisdom learned. Whatever it is, be assured that there are very real emotional reasons for someone wanting to record a life story.

4. Retell your clients' stories.

In retelling your clients' stories you not only demonstrate that you're a good listener but you also help reinforce your clients' "right brain" reasons for wanting to record a life story. As Michael Bosworth says,

> *Then, and only then, are you ready to sell, because then you can retell the customer story with a different ending or a new sequel, with your offering playing a role in the story. It's also useful to have a quiver of "here's how I've helped other*

people" stories, so that you can help the prospect visualize a future that includes you and your offering.

50 5 Tips to Overcoming Your Marketing Blues

Do you ever have what I like to call the marketing blues? It's not pretty.

For me, it starts with a gnawing sense that it's time to get out from behind my computer and let more people know about my services. I know all the marketing stuff I'm supposed to be doing—networking, writing articles, asking for references, making presentations, yadda, yadda, yadda.

But it all seems overwhelming. Where to start? Who to call? What to write? In no time my "Inner Critic" starts berating me. "Who would want *your* personal history services? Who said *you* could market yourself? Others have far more experience than *you* do." Before you know it, I'm back behind my computer feeling defeated, discouraged, and blue.

So how do I get over my "Marketing Blues"? These are the things that work for me. Maybe they'll help you.

Turn off your "Inner Critic."
Simply tell it to get lost. Imagine locking your Critic up in a box and shipping it off to a deserted island. Or come up with your own method of cutting it loose. A great little book I recommend is *Taming Your Gremlin* by Rick Carson.

Do *one* marketing task in *one* hour.

Pick one simple thing you can do in the next hour. Don't worry about whether it fits some larger marketing plan or whether your "Inner Critic" pops back to tell how silly you're being. For me, it can be sending a note and card to some former clients. In it I wish them a Happy Fall or Happy Spring, whatever's appropriate. I briefly tell them what I'm up to and wish them well. Sometimes I'll set aside an hour to learn something new about marketing. The point is to do one marketing task in an hour.

Reread a favorite marketing book.

One of my favorites is Jeffrey Gitomer's *Little Red Book of Selling*. It's only 219 pages. I can open it up anywhere and get great advice and motivation.

Make a date with a positive, successful friend.

I have a friend who, unlike me, is an extrovert with boundless energy. She's very successful at her home-based business. Getting together—not to have a pity party, but to generate ideas with her—is a great antidote for my blues.

Make an action list.

I write down a list of five marketing things I can do the next day. These are manageable, limited, enjoyable action steps I can accomplish in a day. The next morning I've got a plan in front of me and I'm ready to start.

51 8 Lessons My Mom Taught Me About Marketing

My mom was a wise woman. She never had much schooling but she earned her doctorate at the university of life. She had a homespun wisdom that on reflection has taught me some vital marketing lessons. Here they are:

1. Never leave home without being carefully groomed.

My mom always left her home neatly dressed and with her hair carefully coiffed. When I'm out in my community, I occasionally encounter former clients or workshop participants. Sometimes I find myself talking to a stranger about my work. I'm aware that I'm a walking billboard for personal history. This means I need to look appropriately professional. No need for a suit and tie. But slouching around in sweat pants and ratty sneakers won't do when you're in the public eye.

2. Don't forget to say thank you.

It's a small word that goes a long way to creating a good impression. My mom never failed to say thank you for a kindness shown her. She always sent a thank you card after receiving a gift. Make it a point in your marketing to thank clients. I send a note thanking a potential client even if we don't end up working together. I also send birthday and holiday cards to former clients. It's a special touch that people appreciate and remember.

3. Don't waste time on ungrateful people.

Mom was sweet but she was also strong. If people didn't show some reciprocal kindness or interest, she'd drop them. There's a good marketing lesson here. There's no point trying to promote your personal history services to people who aren't interested or don't care. It's better to concentrate your energy where you're likely to get the best response.

4. Answer letters immediately.

Mom was from a generation of letter writers. Up until her death, she still penned several letters a week to friends and family. And what's crucial is that she never let a week pass before answering a letter. People appreciated her promptness. In marketing our services it's vital to respond to queries in a timely manner. It creates an aura of efficiency, eagerness, and professionalism.

5. Be meticulous.

Mom never let a speck of dust settle on her furniture. Her home was always immaculate. The marketing lesson is that all your print, audio-video, and website materials must be carefully designed and first class.

6. Monday is laundry day.

Mom never multitasked. Each day of the week was set aside for specific chores whether it was laundry, baking, cleaning, or gardening. It's easy to become hit-and-miss with our marketing. Make sure you schedule marketing time each week and stick to it. Better yet, why not make Monday your marketing day?

7. Be frugal and avoid debt.

Mom was a child of the Great Depression. She never spent money she didn't have and always looked for bargains and sales. She's passed that fiscal conservatism on to me. I look for the most cost efficient ways to market my services. For example, my website/blog costs me all of twenty bucks a year. I avoid "gadgets" and constant upgrading and use my equipment and software as long as it still does the job.

8. Don't put on airs.
Mom couldn't abide pretentiousness or arrogance. There's a good marketing lesson here. Avoid overselling or hyping your services. People can smell phoniness a mile off.

Thanks, Mom. You've taught me well.

52 Lousy at Getting Referrals? Here's Some Help.

I've a confession to make. I'm not great at asking for referrals. I usually end up mumbling something lame to my clients like, "If you know of anyone who might like to use my services, please let them know about me." That's it. Then I'm out the door.

I decided it was time to get my act together and do a better job. I've been doing some research on referral strategies and here's what I've learned. I hope you'll find it helps you as well.

Don't forget to ask.
The best time to ask for a referral is when you've delivered your book or video to your clients and they're thrilled with your work.

Develop a large network of referral partners.

In addition to your own clients, think of five to ten occupations that deal with the same clients as personal historians such as: financial planners, home care services for seniors, accountants, funeral directors, professional genealogists, naturopaths, and so on. Now select ten people from each category and arrange to meet them so that you can describe your services and learn more about what they offer. When you find people who are prepared to refer clients to you, add them to your referral partners list. In time you can build a referral list with fifty or more names. Make sure to follow up with your network every three months or so.

Be active in your community.

Make a point of joining business associations and community groups. Your participation will in time lead to referrals.

Provide referrals.

Giving referrals for others is likely to generate in-kind referrals from those you've helped.

Make yourself a low risk referral.

Let's face it. People don't want to take a chance on referring someone they don't know very well. They stand to lose if you screw up. People want assurances. Here's what you need to do.

- *Give your referrers the resources they need.* Make it easy for them by leaving behind some business cards and brochures.
- *Don't be vague about the type of client you want.* It will help if you give them an accurate picture of your ideal client. You might say

something like, "I'm looking for clients who are professional women in their 50s who have one or both parents still living."

- *Be clear about what you expect.* Do you want them to set up a meeting with just you and the prospective client? Or would you like them to be there as well? Is it OK to use their names when calling referred clients?

53 You Can Do It! Get Referral Partners Today

In another article, *Lousy at Getting Referrals? Here's Some Help* (52), I provided several tips that could increase your referrals. A personal historian colleague asked me to expand on my suggestion of developing a large network of referral partners. She asked, "I know that we can benefit one another, but how do they know? How do I persuade them to give me their time for free? And what does it mean to follow up with my network every three months or so?"

Here then is an elaboration on my earlier article on referral partners that I hope addresses my colleague's questions.

This is a long-term process.

You're involved in developing mutually supportive business relationships. It will take time, trust, and patience and not all your efforts will bear fruit. If you're looking for a quick fix, this isn't it.

Create your "ideal client" referral document.

It's helpful to compose a sketch of your perfect client and the follow-up approach you'll use with each referred client. For example, will you contact your referral by telephone, letter, or e-mail? How will you introduce yourself? How will you describe your referral partner's role? Will you send promotional materials or wait until you have a positive response? Will you meet with referrals in their home or in some neutral location like a coffee shop? This document will clarify who you're looking for and it will provide your referral partners with a good overview of your referral strategy. Don't forget to add a few testimonials to your paper.

Identify a referral partner.

Start by choosing a business that likely serves similar clients as personal historians. Make it easy for yourself by identifying a professional you already use and like. Perhaps you know a financial adviser, accountant, or chiropractor that would be willing to be a referral partner. Once you've established this professional as a willing partner, you can ask for names of others he or she would let you contact.

Try the "reverse introduction."

Over at the *Duct Tape Marketing Blog*, John Jantsch has a clever approach to starting a referral partnership. He calls it the *Perfect Introduction in Reverse*. Basically the idea is to start by contacting a potential partner, explaining that you have clients that could benefit from her service or product. It's easier to start when you are *offering* something of value. For example, I've been in touch with a company that provides a complete package of services to assist seniors with moving. It's still early but with time the potential for referrals is there.

Build a trusting relationship.

Keeping referral partners is a matter of building professional trust. You want to be certain that clients you send to your partner are going to have a positive experience. Similar concerns exist for your partner. There are several ways you can go about developing trust. For instance:

- Offer a free seminar for your partner's clients. Invite your referral partner to do the same for you.
- Write an article for your partner's newsletter or website and ask for your partner to write something for your clients.

Keep in touch.

It's important to nurture and care for the professional relationship you develop with your referral partners. Here are some things you can do:

- Send a card or gift for every referral you receive.
- Participate in their charity events.
- Make regular phone calls.
- Send an article that's relevant to their work.

In a nutshell then, getting referral partners is not about asking people to give you something for free. It's about a mutually supportive relationship where each partner wins. And to make certain that the partnership is maintained, you have to find ways to keep in touch.

54 The Introvert's 12 Step Plan for Painless Networking

I am an introvert. The idea of attending a function with a crush of chattering people is about as much fun as sticking needles in my eyes. Now don't get me wrong. I'm not shy. It's just that I get my strength from quiet times away from people.

So how do I deal with the inevitable challenge of attending networking events? While it's still not my favorite thing to do, it's become easier over the years. Here are a few tricks I've learned.

1. Set a goal of talking to three or four people.
Networking isn't a competition to see who can collect the most business cards. What's important is to develop relationships that last. Decide ahead of time the minimum number of people you'll talk to before leaving the event. Over time you might gain the confidence to eventually set a higher goal.

2. Start small.
Do one or two functions a month and choose smaller groups where you won't feel overwhelmed.

3. Think of it as building relationships.
You want to take the time to have conversations with people in order to create some long-term connections that can be mutually beneficial.

4. Be helpful.

Remember it's not about selling yourself. It's about helping people. Perhaps it's making a connection or recommendation for someone. Or maybe it's sending the person a useful article.

5. Pretend you've organized the event.

Whenever I organize an event, I feel great. As host I'm free to make sure people are comfortable, make introductions, and see to the loners in the crowd. Now I take this mindset with me when I attend a networking event. The mental shift from guest to host frees me up and I enjoy myself more. Try it. It works!

6. Seek out those who are on their own.

Remember you're there to be helpful. What better way to help than to strike up a conversation with someone who looks lost and uncomfortable. The person's probably a fellow introvert!

7. Break the ice.

It's not important what you say. It's small talk. Comment on the weather, food, the crowd, or the season. Don't keep the small talk going too long. If there's some rapport, then shift to more substantial questions.

8. Ask questions and listen.

This should be pretty easy for personal historians. Ask open-ended questions like, "What brings you here today? How long have you been with this organization? What do you like about your work? " Listen carefully and focus on your guest. Don't let your gaze wander over the crowd.

9. Play to your strengths.

You're an introvert. Most introverts are pretty good listeners. Don't pretend to be an extrovert. You'll look phony and feel horrible in the process.

10. Don't sell.

People don't come to networking events to be pitched products or services. It's annoying. When asked what you do, have a succinct and clear statement about how your service helps people. It might be something like, "I'm a personal historian. I record and preserve family stories. My clients are often sons and daughters who want to record their parents' lives but are too busy to do it themselves."

11. Move on.

We introverts can find it difficult to break away from a conversation. But really it's not that hard. Most who attend a networking function expect people to mingle. No need to make an excuse. When you know it's time to move on simple say, "I've enjoyed talking to you. I really appreciate what you have to say about…[fill in the blank]. May I have your business card?"

12. Reward yourself.

Before your networking gig think of a way to reward yourself for stepping up to the plate. Maybe it's playing hooky one afternoon and seeing a movie. Or perhaps it's going for a relaxing massage. You know what works for you. Just be sure to do it!

55 Attention Introverts! You Can Market Successfully!

Another article of mine, *The Introvert's 12 Step Plan for Painless Networking* (54), hit a chord among my fellow introverts. This got me thinking that marketing for introverts was a natural follow-up.

Like most introverts I'm not shy, but I need time alone to restore my energy. Crowds tire me out. I prefer one-on-one conversations to cocktail parties. I need time to plan and think. I'm a good listener and good at getting others to talk. For years I saw these traits as counterproductive when it came to marketing. But not anymore.

Here's what I've learned about marketing successfully as an introvert.

Be yourself.
Being an introvert is not a character flaw. Your introvert qualities are a marketing advantage. Don't try to take on a false extroverted persona. It'll wear you out and drive people away. Bill Gates and Steven Spielberg did it their way and you guessed it, they're introverts!

Meet one-on-one.
Avoid crowds. Meet someone over coffee or lunch. Have colleagues and friends suggest the names of people you might contact.

Keep in touch.
Marketing is about establishing relationships. Introverts excel at meaningful conversations so keep in touch with your contacts because it's easier than making new ones.

Write rather than call.

If you find a cold call has your stomach churning, write a letter or send an e-mail instead. It may not be as effective as a telephone call but it's much better than no contact at all.

Publish.

Writing is an introvert's best friend. Start writing articles, newsletters, blog posts, or books. Clients will get to know you through your writing and be drawn to your services.

Engage a buddy.

There's nothing in the rules that says you have to market alone. Engaging the world is easier with a supportive colleague. Bring someone along to your next networking event.

Solve, don't sell.

No one likes a sales pitch. We are badgered daily by the hard sell. Do what introverts do best: listen. Remember you don't have to brag to market successfully. By carefully listening and asking the right questions you can point your client toward solutions that naturally use your skills and talent.

Prepare.

Like most introverts I like to think before I act. I find it helpful to prepare ahead before going to a mixer or making informational telephone calls. I make a list of questions or topics that I want to cover on an index card so I have it for ready reference. It's not that I use the card that often but knowing it's close at hand gives me some security.

56   10 Ways to Ensure Your Marketing Fails

Previously I wrote about *12 Ways to Ensure Your Personal History Business Fails* (25). One of my tips in that article was "Stop Marketing." I'd like to expand on that and look at how to *fail totally* at marketing. Heck, without marketing you won't have to deal with all those pesky clients. More time to sit back and relax!

Follow my 10 tips and you're on your way to stress-free living!

1. Avoid meeting potential clients.
This is the key tip. If people don't know you exist, they'll never bother to use your services.

2. Spend months researching how to market.
I love research. There's no better way to learn a lot and do absolutely nothing. The upside is that you can easily convince yourself that you're really doing something. Perfect!

3. Use the wrong marketing approach.
We all know that personal history clients like to get up close and personal. They want to be sure they can trust you with their stories. So avoid contact at all costs. Instead, spend your marketing budget on advertisements in newspapers and magazines. Talk about why you have a great product/service and don't mention anything about yourself.

4. Turn down public speaking requests.

(See Tip 1: Avoid meeting potential clients.) Putting yourself in a roomful of people is an open invitation for someone to ask about your services. Now that could be a problem!

5. Don't mention what you do.

Refrain from casually talking about your work when out in public or among friends and colleagues. You never want to be put on the spot by people telling you they have the perfect client for you. Remember it's all about avoiding clients!

6. Prepare elaborate marketing plans.

This flows nicely from Tip 2: Spend months researching. The trick here is to design something so detailed and complex that you'll be too exhausted thinking about it to do anything.

7. Don't network. Marketing gurus are big on networking.

Really, it's just a lot of mingling with strangers in the hopes of making some useful connections in the future. Your goal is to fail now *and* in the future. Don't be seduced by expert opinion!

8. Forget social media.

I know blogging, Facebook, and Twitter are all the rage. But it'll only get you noticed. Remember Tip 1. Forget about publishing a blog. And if you do have one, then make sure your posts are infrequent and devoid of anything useful.

9. Confuse potential clients.

If you do have the misfortune of encountering a real client, confuse them. At all costs avoid asking what they want. Talk nonstop about the variety of personal histories that can be produced; the different costs for each type of product; the advantages and disadvantages of print versus video; the length of time it takes to record stories; and the equipment you use. If you're successful, you should be able to drive away not only this client but anyone else she talks to about your service.

10. Believe that marketing is "sleazy."

Think about late-night infomercials, and you'll be sufficiently appalled that marketing will totally turn you off. If you need help, just watch a few!

57 What Do Fishing and Personal History Clients Have in Common?

When I was a young lad, an old friend of the family would sometimes take me fishing. He was a good fisherman and he would always say, "Dan, if you want to catch fish, you've got to go where the fish are." This got me thinking that you could apply this piece of folk wisdom to marketing. *If you want to get personal history clients, you've got to go where the personal history clients are.*

Marketing experts stress the importance of knowing your target audience. Over the years I realize that my clients tend to have somewhat the same profile. And this profile rings true for many other personal historians. For the most part my clients are:

- Female
- Professional
- 50 to 60 years old
- at least one parent living
- Wanting to record and preserve a parent's life story
- Too busy or lacking the skill to produce a personal history

Like fishing, knowing who your clients are helps determine how and where you might reach them. If you want to find some personal history clients who meet the profile above, I'd suggest the following:

- Join a professional networking group like BNI (Business Network International), Chamber of Commerce, or eWomenNetwork.
- Write an article or get interviewed for the Lifestyle section of your local newspaper.
- Participate in community groups like fitness and yoga classes, choirs, and adult education classes.
- Join or offer presentations to women's professional associations and groups.
- Become involved with your Alumni association.
- Join and participate in Facebook and Twitter groups that have an interest in family stories.

58 What's the Connection Between Reflexology and Life Stories?

I visited my local vitamin shop last week and ended up sampling a free, ten-minute reflexology treatment. My feet felt wonderful. This got me thinking. Reflexologists and personal historians face the same marketing challenge. People have heard about us but don't really know what we're about.

Samples help people make purchasing decisions. So I plan to include some free samples as part of my personal history marketing repertoire in the new year. Here's what I've decided to do. You can try out my plan for yourself or adapt it and see what happens.

The plan. I'll suggest to my neighborhood bookstore that I'd like to spend a day offering interested patrons a free, ten-minute, digitally recorded life story interview. The interviews, I'll explain, will be conducted in a quiet corner and will not interfere with the normal flow of customers.

The execution. I'll have some ten-minute topics to suggest to a willing patron such as: *Who was the biggest influence in your life? What are some important life lessons you've learned? What's your favorite childhood memory?*

After the interview, I'll download the recording and burn a CD on the spot. I'll tuck it into a protective sleeve or case and hand it to my interviewee, along with a brochure that outlines the benefits and services I provide. Prior to the sample sessions, I'll burn a label on the CDs that includes a title, such as *Memories* and my name and contact information.

How will people find me? There are a couple of possibilities. I'll encourage the bookstore staff to mention my free offer. If space permits, I'll set up a chair with a sign above me that reads.

> *Preserving Memories Is An Act of Love. Get your free mini-memoir recorded here.*

A footnote. Because the sample interview is a free offering, I want to keep my costs and time to a minimum. That's why I'm planning to download and burn CDs on the spot. This ensures that at a later date I don't have to deliver or mail out CDs. Besides, the interviewees will appreciate being able to take away their mini-memoir immediately.

59 How to Ace Your Next Media Interview.

I've given countless interviews for both local and national media outlets. What I've learned, I've condensed into these handy tips that I hope will be of some help. (Please note that the radio and TV tips assume that you'll be doing a studio interview. Even if you're not, the rules still hold for an "on location" interview.)

General tips for all media interviews:
- *Use anecdotes.* Come up with a short story (about 30 seconds) to illustrate your point. Remember, humor works well.

- *Think of some likely questions you'll be asked.* Then prepare some pointed facts and brief stories you can use.
- *Don't rehearse.* Many "experts" suggest rehearsing—and they're wrong! Doing so can make you feel more stressful because you'll be worried about getting it right.
- *Study your interviewer.* Take time to catch several episodes of the host's show. You'll get a sense of the person's style and approach. If you're being interviewed for a magazine or newspaper, read a few articles the journalist has written.
- *Don't use professional jargon.* Use simple, everyday words.
- *Don't rush to your interview.* At least a day in advance, learn where the TV or radio studio is located and find the best route to get there. On the day of the interview, leave extra time for getting to it. You want to be as relaxed as possible, not tense from cutting the time too close.

Tips for TV interviews:

- *Focus on your host.* Make a connection with the interviewer and don't look at the camera. You're talking to one person, not thousands. This will help you remain calm.
- *Wear solid colors and avoid anything flashy.* You want the audience to be fascinated by what you're saying, not what you're wearing. Avoid stripes or busy patterns. The camera doesn't like them. Use black, blinding white, and bright red sparingly.
- *Ask ahead how much time you'll have.* "On Air" time is often short; think five minutes or less. Make sure you have two or three points you really want to stress. Insert these into whatever question you're asked.

- *Bring props.* Television loves visuals. Offer the TV producer a 30- or 60-second clip of your videos. If you produce books, bring samples.
- *Smile.* Avoid at all cost the "deer in the headlights" syndrome. Have some fun.

Tips for radio interviews:

- *Appearance.* It's less important than for TV. However, this doesn't mean showing up in your track suit. Wear comfortable, but appropriate, professional attire.
- *Bring notes.* It's radio so you can't be seen! Jot on an index card three key points you want to make.
- *Avoid a monotone voice.* All the listener has to go on is the sound of your voice. Keep it conversational, but be conscious of expressing yourself with some passion.

Tips for newspaper and magazine interviews:

- *Have contact names.* A journalist will likely want to talk to some of your clients. Make sure you have the names and contact information for two or three of your clients. Try to go for variety—younger, older, male, female. Get your clients' approval beforehand to use their names.
- *Have samples.* It helps to be able to show some of your work.

60 How to Get Control of Your Pre-Presentation Jitters

I'm a "ham" at heart so I love to get in front of an audience, big or small. But when it comes to an important presentation where I know I've got to make a good impression, I can feel the pre-presentation jitters creeping in. Over the years I've learned some practical steps to calm myself. Try these the next time you've got to make a "big" presentation.

Know your stuff.
The best way to keep the jitters at bay is to be well prepared. Practice your presentation in front of a friend and get some constructive feedback.

Arrive early.
Nothing adds more to your anxiety than rushing madly to get to your presentation on time. Check Google Maps for the best route from your place to the venue where you'll be speaking.

Do a room check.
If possible, check out the room prior to your presentation. Make sure that the equipment you requested is in place and works. Is the seating arranged in a suitable manner for your talk? Is the room at a comfortable temperature?

Mingle.
I find this a real tension buster. If you have a chance, move about the room and introduce yourself to people who've come to hear you. When

you get up to talk, you'll feel that you're talking to individuals, not a big, amorphous group.

Don't forget to breathe.
Before starting your presentation, check your breathing. Chances are it'll be somewhat shallow. Take several deliberate, deep, slow breaths and you'll find it helps to relax you.

Go slow.
Nothing broadcasts nervousness more than a speaker who breathlessly rushes into his presentation and never stops. Be focused, deliberate, and slow at the outset.

61 Should I Have a Business Blog?

That's the question that rattled around in my head some years ago. So I started reading everything that I could lay my hands on about blogging. I discovered, among other things, that blogging could be a very useful business tool.

I decided to take the plunge in 2008 and set up my blog. What I've learned might be useful to those of you still thinking about doing so. I'm not a Web 2.0 expert and I'm not going to tell you that blogging will bring you fame and fortune. But I hope you'll see that blogging can be an important part of your personal history business.

Seven reasons why you need a business blog.
1. Millions of people every day search for information and services on the Internet. If you're not there, they won't find you.

2. Blogs are easier and cheaper to set up and maintain than websites. I spent all of $20 getting my WordPress blog launched.

3. Google ranks blogs higher on its listing than web pages. Search engines like activity and links. If you post frequently and people link to your blog, you'll eventually be on page one of Google.

4. Blogs are more personal and informal than a website. They allow for conversations, and in our business being personal is a critical part of who we are.

5. Blogs can establish you as an authority. Part of this has to do with publishing content regularly. As Woody Allen said, "80% of success is showing up."

6. Blogs are a great way to connect with clients and share valuable content about life stories.

7. Writing on a regular basis clarifies your thinking and adds immeasurably to your learning about the many facets of personal history.

Has blogging worked for me? It has. At the end of my fifth year I had nearly 400 subscribers, and 321,643 visitors. I had written 704 posts and received 1,496 comments. I consistently appeared in the top five Google listings for "personal historian."

I also discovered how much I enjoyed writing articles and how it limbered up my creativity and worked my "writing muscles." I've come to know some of my personal history colleagues better and expanded my network to include genealogists, social-networkers, and writers.

So what do you say? Time to take the plunge?

62 What Everybody Ought to Know About a Successful Blog

If you want a blog that will attract and keep readers, then this is what you need to do.

Post frequently.

Aim for at least one post a week. Writing once a month won't attract and hold visitors to your blog. The exception to this rule would be an original, dynamite, and must-have article each time. Then once a month might work.

Be consistent.

As Woody Allen said, "Eighty percent of success is showing up." Visitors to your blog want to know that they can count on you to deliver.

Be personal.

The best blogs are those that give you a real sense of the person behind the articles. Write conversationally. To illustrate a point, use your own experience. A word of caution: don't write only about yourself. Unless your life is truly riveting, most people really don't care.

Keep it short and scan-able.

The truth is that visitors to a web page don't stay long. As a rule they want quick, relevant information, presented clearly and succinctly. So use bulleted lists, short paragraphs, headings, and sub headings.

Keep it uncluttered.

You want to make it easy for visitors to find their way around your blog. You don't need to hire an expensive website designer. Many of the existing blog templates work well. Just don't load them down with too much stuff.

Use photographs.

Photos add interest. They can attract attention to your content and leaven longer articles.

Use catchy headlines.

Think newspapers and popular magazines when writing your headlines. You want them to be simple, intriguing, and descriptive.

Be generous and useful.

Don't hoard your best ideas. Create useful reports and give them away for free. Keep your audience in mind and solve problems they're encountering.

For more on successful blogging these two sites are terrific: *ProBlogger* and *Copyblogger*.

63 4 Tips to Keep Your Blog Fresh, Consistent, and Enduring.

I've been asked, "How do you keep a blog going and keep it fresh, regular, and on time? It's a skill I can't seem to master yet!"

After years of blogging, I learned what kept me going.

Find your passion.
Writing regularly requires passion. If you don't have enthusiasm and interest for your material, writing will be laborious and you'll resent putting in the time.

I'm naturally curious and I enjoy researching and writing. This combined with my love of life stories made producing for my blog a delight—well, most of the time. ;-)

Finding your passion is easier said than done. Here's a clue. What is it that you love and can't wait to do? What do you find yourself doing when other more pragmatic things require your attention?

Know your audience.
It's difficult to come up with material if you don't have an audience in mind.

When I started my blog, my focus was split between the hobbyist doing life stories and the professional personal historian. It didn't work. After several months I knew that the people I wanted to write for were like me—professional personal historians working at their craft full-time.

So ask yourself, "Who are the people I really want to talk to?"

Think outside the box.
Coming up with fresh original material week after week can be challenging. One method of sparking article content is combining apparently non-related subjects. For example, I used my cat to come up

with *6 Lessons My Cat Taught Me About Time Management* (11). Betty White became the inspiration for *What Betty White Can Teach You About Your Personal History Business* (29). And my garden provided fodder for *What Gardening Can Teach You About Growing Your Business* (14).

Other sources I went to regularly for inspiration were newspaper and magazine articles, movies, other blogs, forums, Facebook, and Twitter. After a while your radar is alert for potential blog articles in the most unlikely places. Coming out of my neighborhood bank one day, I saw a sign that led to this article, *Are Your Clients Extremely Satisfied With Your Services?* (39).

Be self-disciplined.

If you're going to be consistent with your blog posts, you need to be disciplined. It doesn't matter whether you write one post a week or five. What matters to your readers is that they can count on you being there. Consistency demonstrates that you take your blog seriously.

Schedule blog time in your work week calendar making certain to book an uninterrupted hour or two. Try to select periods in the day when you naturally have more energy.

Avoid distractions. Close your Internet browser, let your answering service pick up your calls, and close the door to your office. Don't get up from your desk until you've spent at least 30 minutes researching or writing.

Conclusion.

If you have something to say and you want to build a readership for your blog, you've got to work at it. Don't expect immediate results. It'll take a couple of years before you start to see the fruits of your labor.

When I started out, I barely averaged 600 viewers a month. Five years later I reached over 300,000 visitors a year. True, it's a small number when compared to such mega star blogs as Zen Habits and copyblogger. Then again, the personal historian niche is small and I was pleased with my progress.

64 How to Turn Your Blog Posts Into an E-Book

Want to give all those blog articles you've written a second life? I certainly do.

I've assembled five online services that allow you to do just that by capturing blog articles and editing them into an e-book.

Here's my take on these services. I really like *Anthologize* but it isn't compatible with blogs like mine that operate on WordPress.com. *Ebook Glue* downloads your whole blog and doesn't appear to allow for editing. *Papyrus* only works with Chrome and Safari browsers and I use Firefox. I didn't want to download a different browser just to use their program.

This leaves me with two services—*BookSmith* and *Zinepal*. Both look relatively easy to use.

- Anthologize (http://anthologize.org/) "...a free, open-source, plugin that transforms WordPress into a platform for publishing electronic texts. Grab posts from your WordPress blog, import feeds from external sites, or create new content directly within Anthologize. Then outline, order, and edit your work, crafting it into a single volume for export in several formats, including—in this release—PDF, ePUB, TEI. *Please note that Anthologize cannot be installed on blogs hosted at WordPress.com.*"
- BookSmith (http://blog2book.pothi.com/app/) "...a tool that lets you convert your blog posts into print ready book files easily and quickly. We currently support following platforms: Blogger.com (hosted on blogspot.com or elsewhere) and WordPress (self hosted as well as WordPress MU platforms like those on wordpress.com)."
- Ebook Glue (https://ebookglue.com/) "...was developed in late 2012, and was launched on December 24, 2012. Since then, over 2,000 blogs have used Ebook Glue to publish their content as a downloadable ebook."
- Papyrus. (http://papyruseditor.com/) "...gives you a very simple online editing interface to create your books. Convert your blog to a book in one click."
- Zinepal: (http://www.zinepal.com/how) "...creates eBooks in the PDF, ePub, Kindle and Mobipocket formats. It's one of the easiest ways to make eBooks and printable PDFs from existing web content in order to reach additional audiences and offer readers more choices."

65 8 Reasons Why Personal Historians Should Use Twitter

[A tip of the hat to Diane Haddad at *Genealogy Insider* for giving me the idea for this article.]

These days there's a lot in the news about Twitter. Some of you might be tempted to dismiss it as a fad and of little value to you as a personal historian. I've been using Twitter for a while and see its potential. Here are eight reasons why I think you should give it a try:

1. Expand your network.

Open up to a whole new group of personal and family historians. Go to the search box on Twitter and enter "family stories" or "life stories." All kinds of folks will pop up who have some connection to these topics. When you've found some people to follow, check out who they're following. You might want to follow some of these people as well.

2. Drive traffic to your blog or website.

The Google search engines like activity. The more they see, the more your site will rank higher on Google pages. You can feed your blog posts to your Twitter account and attract a whole new group of readers. I've noticed a definite increase in visitors to my blog since I started using Twitter.

3. Get great ideas.

Many bloggers (including yours truly) find a wealth of ideas for material to write about in their blog. In addition, there are creative ways that people are preserving family stories—ways that you might never have considered.

4. Ask questions.
Twitter is a good way to get some feedback. You can ask a question of all your followers or direct it to one person using @ and their user name like this: @dancurtis.

5. Find how-to advice.
There are lots of great tips and links to useful online articles.

6. Be on top of the latest personal history news.
Twitter is a huge interconnected web with millions of users picking up news and often "Retweeting" it before a story hits the newsstand or airwaves.

7. Find bargains.
Whether it's travel, supplies, or equipment there are great deals and giveaways often exclusive to Twitter users. You can go to Twitter search and type in **#bargains** where you'll find a goldmine that would warm the heart of any "shopaholic."

8. Your own "virtual" water cooler.
If you work from home, it can sometimes be lonely. With Twitter you can jump in at any time of the day and follow the conversations or join in yourself. It can break the sense of isolation that can too easily be part of self-employment.

CHAPTER 5:
What I Tell Prospective Clients

66 See How Easily You Can Write Your Life Story

How many of you have sat down with the best of intentions to write your life story? Or have tried to get someone else to write theirs? I'm continually encountering people who started writing several years ago and haven't progressed much beyond their first chapter.

Why is that?

Well there are several reasons. Sometimes it's just a matter of finding the time. Many people today are suffering from time deprivation. Trying to fit one more thing into a busy schedule seems impossible. For others, sitting alone at a desk and composing sentences is a chore. The words just don't seem to come. Some people don't know where to start. Should I organize my life story chronologically or thematically? Should I include my ancestors or just my immediate family?

So if you find yourself nodding in agreement with what I've just said, here's a solution. Hire a professional personal historian. You can find someone in your area by going to the website of the Association of Personal Historians.

Here are seven benefits to hiring a personal historian.

1. A personal historian can manage your print and video project from beginning to end. No need for you to learn all kinds of new software programs.
2. Being interviewed by a personal historian who is an empathetic listener is more engaging than working on your own.
3. Talking to a neutral, non-family member can be easier than being interviewed by a friend or relative.
4. Personal historians are skilled at asking just the right questions to bring out comprehensive and nuanced stories.
5 A personal historian can help edit your story and bring clarity and "readability" to your work.
6. A personal historian can ensure that your story will be preserved in a professional and attractive manner.
7. Lastly, and most importantly your life story will get done.

67 5 Benefits of Hiring a Personal Historian

If you're thinking of hiring a personal historian, keep reading. If you're a practicing personal historian, remember that potential clients don't really care *what you do*. What they care about are the *benefits* they'll get from hiring you.

I must admit that I sometimes forget this fact. So as a reminder to myself and to anyone else who needs a prompt about the benefits—here are five important ones.

1. Your story will get told.

This is the most important benefit of all. Countless times people have told me that they started working on their life story or that of a family member but never seemed to be able to get it finished. Hiring a personal historian means the work will get done on time and in a professional manner.

2. It's more fun.

Let's face it, sitting alone with a blank computer screen or piece of paper and waiting for inspiration to strike can be daunting. We are by nature conversationalists. Sitting with a personal historian who is a skilled interviewer and empathetic listener makes telling your story an enjoyable experience.

3. Your story will be richer in detail.

Because of the familiarity with your own story, you can easily miss details that others would find fascinating. You need a personal historian who is fresh to your story and has the skill to bring out the richness of your life's journey.

4. A personal historian relieves you of the burden of producing your book.

Putting together a life story is an overwhelming undertaking for most people. From start to finish it requires a set of skills that include interviewing, editing, research, photo enhancement, design and layout, and printing. A personal historian takes on these production tasks and ensures that all are handled professionally.

5. A personal historian has the time.

Are you someone who simply can't find enough hours in a day to devote to working on your own story or that of a family member? Hiring a personal historian relieves you of the guilt of not putting in the time you need to get your life story or that of a family member told.

68 How to Find a Personal Historian

Let's say you've decided you really need help getting your personal history completed or you want someone to produce a personal history of your mother. Where do you find a personal historian? Here are several suggestions that should help you in your search:

- *The Association of Personal Historians,* an international organization with over 700 members located primarily in North America (www.personalhistorians.org). If you go to their site, you can search for a personal historian in your region. The APH is not a governing body and doesn't set pricing or professional guidelines so for some guidance refer to other articles, *How Much*

Should You Pay A Personal Historian? (70) *and 9 Questions to Ask Before Hiring A Personal Historian* (69).

- *Google search:* Type in any of the following key word combinations —personal historian, your life story, family stories —and you'll see an extensive listing of personal historian blogs and web sites.
- *Community centers/libraries:* A number of personal historians offer workshops and courses on writing your personal history through such places. You might contact your local community center or library to ask if they know of any personal historians in your area.
- *Referrals:* Most personal historians are happy to refer you to their colleagues. So if you can't locate a personal historian in your community, go to the APH site and get the names of several personal historians who live nearest to you. Contact them and ask if they might know a local personal historian.
- *Social media:* More personal historians are using networks such as Facebook, Twitter, and LinkedIn. Go to any of these services and search for "personal historian" and you'll likely find someone.

69 9 Questions to Ask Before Hiring a Personal Historian

I wrote about the advantages of using the services of a personal historian in another article (Tip 67). I'd like to focus on nine questions you need to ask before hiring a personal historian. There are no professional bodies that certify or oversee personal historians. Anyone can hang up a shingle that says "personal historian." So it's buyer beware.

1. Does the personal historian belong to any professional associations?

Belonging to an association such as the Association of Personal Historians, the Oral History Association, or the National Storytelling Association is important. It means the personal historian takes his work seriously as a professional. Associations provide their members with opportunities to learn more and improve their skills.

2. Does the personal historian have samples of her work?

Even if a personal historian is just starting out, she needs to be able to show you a book or video that she has completed. You want to be able to assess the quality of her work.

3. Is the personal historian open to having you talk to previous clients about their experience?

It's useful to get previous client's evaluations. While it's not foolproof, it does allow you to have a better feeling for the person you may hire.

4. Does the personal historian operate in a professional manner?

Does she show up for appointments on time? Does he have a contract that spells out precisely what each stage of the production will entail and how fees are to be calculated? Does she answer all your queries in a prompt, courteous, and clear manner? Does he refrain from pressure tactics?

5. Do you feel comfortable around this person?

Whether you're hiring a personal historian for yourself or another family member, you want to feel at ease. It will not be an enjoyable experience if you end up spending many hours with someone you don't like.

6. Before becoming a personal historian, what was the person's previous work experience?

Personal historians come from all kinds of work backgrounds. But it's fair to say that many come with experience in the humanities. It's not uncommon to find former journalists, filmmakers, editors, librarians, and teachers now working as personal historians. There are exceptions to every rule but you'll likely find a more skilled personal historian coming from the ranks of those who've "apprenticed" in the arts. Someone with little life experience whose previous employment hasn't lent itself to crafting skills in interviewing, writing, and editing may not yet be ready to take on a professional assignment as a personal historian.

7. What is your specialty?

Be leery of anyone who answers, "Oh, I like to work on everything—books, video, audio—you name it!" It's true that there are personal historians who are multi-talented and produce more than one type of product. But even if that is the case, I'd ask what the personal historian enjoys working on the most. Chances are that she will have a preference and if her preference doesn't match yours, then I'd want to see some concrete examples of her work. Bottom line—if you want a book produced, it makes sense to hire someone who has a track record making books. Similarly, if you want a DVD, hire a personal historian whose specialty is video.

8. How long have you been a personal historian?

There isn't a magical number of years of experience that turns someone into a seasoned personal historian. But I'd prefer to hire someone who had been working professionally for at least a couple of years. The longer a personal historian has been working, the more experience he will have and the more samples of his work he will also have for your perusal. On the other hand, if a personal historian is just starting out, you might be able to work out a discount depending on what he's charging.

9. What attracted you to this work?

There isn't any right answer to this question. What you want to be wary of is a reply that sounds too pat, contrived, or rehearsed. Listen for an answer that suggests that this work resonates deeply with this person. For instance, she may have a compelling story to tell about the path that led her to become a personal historian.

70 How Much Should You Pay a Personal Historian?

A common question I get is, "How much would a personal history cost?" I tell people it's a little like going to a car dealer and asking, "How much do your cars cost?" If you're looking at a used economy model, you're going to pay much less than for a luxury sedan. Similarly a personal history can be simple or complex. You could have a 50-page, soft cover booklet detailing a memorable phase in someone's life. Or you could have a 90-minute video biography complete with interviews, family photos and video, music, titles, and effects.

In addition, there are all kinds of personal historians. Some do life stories to add an interesting sideline to their retirement. Other personal historians are hobbyists who work primarily with their own family or friends. There are those who work full time as personal historians and have many years of experience. And there are individuals who are starting up their personal history business and looking to find clients. Within this diverse group charges can vary widely.

Let's look at where the expense comes in. There are essentially eight stages that almost all personal history productions take. They are:

1. Initial consultation to decide what is to be included in the history.
2. Interviewing the subject. This can involve anywhere from 2 to 13 hours or more depending on the scope of the production.
3. Transcribing the interviews in order to edit and construct the story.
4. Editing and shaping the narrative.
5. Searching for appropriate photos, artifacts, videos, sound effects, or music.
6. Completing a rough edit of the book, video or audio.
7. Presenting a copy to the client for review.
8. Final edit and completion of production.

The amount of time it takes to interview someone is actually a small portion of the overall production. As a rough guide, it takes anywhere from 10 to 15 hours of editing for every one hour of interview. Personal historians charge either set package prices, work by the hour, or a combination of both. All professional personal historians will provide you with a contract spelling out the costs and payment stages.

So how much is it going to cost you to have a full-length personal history told? As I mentioned, there are many variables that determine cost. But for argument's sake let's look at one possible example—a video biography. It takes about five to seven hours of interview for a video biography and you can add to that another five to seven hours for travel, set-up of lights, camera, and sound. If a personal historian is charging $40 to $60 an hour, then you're looking at a minimum of $400 up to $840 just in labor to complete a set of interviews. Added to this can be the cost of materials and in the case of a video production, camera, light and sound equipment charges.

Following the interviews comes the editing which takes most of the time. If there are five hours of interview, it's safe to say it will take anywhere from 50 to 75 hours of editing time. If a personal historian is charging $40/hr., then you're looking at somewhere between $2,000 and $3,000 for editing. Added to this can be the costs for editing rooms and equipment. So at the low end of the scale it will cost you anywhere from $2,400 to $3,840 for a 90-minute video biography. Top end can be double those figures or more. Beware of anyone suggesting they can produce a full-scale life history video or book for under $1,000. It can't be done unless that person is offering most of his or her time for free.

I think it's fair to say that most professional personal historians will work within your budget to come up with a life story document that will meet with your approval. It might not be the luxury sedan you'd imagined but rather a nice shiny little compact car. The good news, though, is that unlike cars, which depreciate the moment you take them off the lot, a personal history will gain value over the years. It will in fact become a priceless legacy.

CHAPTER 6:
Dollars & Sense

71 Can I Make a Living as a Personal Historian?

I get asked this question with increasing regularity. And my response is—it depends. Like most things in life, there isn't a simple answer. Here are a few things to ponder.

What do you consider a living wage?

If you need to earn a six-figure salary in order to maintain your lifestyle, you're unlikely to achieve that as a personal historian. I'd suggest you take up cosmetic surgery!

But maybe you're thinking, "I'm looking at a more modest income, maybe around $50,000 a year."

Okay. Let's do the math. On average it takes about three months to complete a personal history book. You might be able to produce four books a year. That means you're going to have to charge your clients $12,500 per book to make $50,000 a year. And remember, you'll have to deduct your business expenses from that figure.

It's great if you can find clients who are willing to pay you that amount. But I'll be frank. While $12,500 is a reasonable price to pay for a personal history, you'll find many potential clients will be shocked by the price.

People love the concept of personal histories, but they haven't a clue about the costs of producing one.

How soon do you need to earn some money?

If you're new to self-employment, you're in for a surprise. It'll take you at least a couple of years of hard work to make your business profitable. Without another source of income or sufficient savings to tide you over, it's almost impossible to reach a point where you're making a living from personal histories.

Do you have the right qualities to be a personal historian?

If you don't have the qualities that are required of a personal historian, you're going to find earning a living from this work a challenge. Here's a check-list of some of those qualities. How do you think you fare?

- excellent interviewing skills
- non-judgmental
- enjoy working alone
- able to market and promote oneself
- patient

- empathetic listener
- self-motivated
- comfortable at public speaking
- proficient writing and editing skills
- love variety
- a positive attitude
- enjoy working with people

How hard are you prepared to work?

Being a personal historian can be a very enjoyable hobby. But if you're intending this to be a business, then be prepared to work harder than you've ever worked before. For the first few years this can means 10 to 12 hour days, 7 day weeks, with few if any holidays. Trust me, I've been there.

Putting in this kind of effort works if you're passionate about what you're doing. But if you don't have that "fire in your belly," then do yourself a favor and don't even start.

Conclusion.

You can make a living being a personal historian provided you've got the right personality, love life stories and people, are prepared to work hard, and aren't looking to earn top dollars.

72 Do You Have a Problem Knowing What to Charge Clients?

For many newcomers to the business of Personal Histories determining what to charge is a challenge. There are no set industry standards and fees range from next to nothing to $100+ an hour.

It doesn't really matter what other personal historians charge for their work. We're all different. One size does not fit all. So here's what to do.

Start with your own expenses. Make a detailed listing of all your expenses for a year. Include everything—personal as well as business. Include a "contingency" amount for such things as health emergencies, repairs, travel, etc. Don't forget taxes and start-up equipment such as printers, scanners, cameras, recorders, etc. Divide your total expenses by 12 to arrive at a monthly estimate.

Let's imagine your calculations point to monthly expenses of $4,000. If your only source of income is from your personal history work, you'll need to generate at least $4,000 of income every month or about $1,000 a week just to meet your expenses.

Calculate your billable hours. Use good time tracking software and determine how much of your time is spent on non-billable activities such as research, marketing, bookkeeping, file management, and so on. A good rule of thumb is 20 percent of your billable hours. So if you work a 40-hour week, you'll be spending about 8 hours a week on non-billable items. This means you need to charge a little more than $30 an hour for the remaining 32 billable hours in order to bring in a $1000 a week (40 hour work week minus 8 hours non-billable items).

Determine your profit margin. Being self-employed means both flush and lean times. To ensure that you can bridge those downturns in your business, build in a profit margin. Consider anything from 10 percent to 30 percent.

Suppose you decide on 15 percent. That would mean adding an additional $4.50 (15 percent of $30) to your hourly rate bringing it to $34.50.

You may prefer to charge by the project. If so, estimate the number of hours to complete a project and multiply by your hourly rate. And don't forget to double the amount of time you think a project will take. It always takes longer than you anticipate.

Avoid pricing yourself too low. Clients might assume you're not good because you're cheap.

Don't base your rate on what others are charging.

You're a professional and are worth every penny you charge.

Additional Resources:

- *Pricing Strategies for Freelancers and Consultants* by Laurie Lewis
- *7 Resources New Freelancers Can Use to Figure Out What to Charge* (http://business.tutsplus.com/articles/freelance-rate-resources--fsw-35423)

73 How to Retain Clients Who Can't Afford You

I'm sure that many of you have had the experience of a potential client eagerly wanting to engage your personal history services but unable to afford the cost. It's disappointing. But here's a word of advice. Don't immediately slash your rates to try to get the job. No self-respecting professional would do that. There's a better way.

As a professional we want to be helpful and we want to be remembered. This client may not be able to afford you but if her experience with you is a positive one and exceeds her expectations, then she'll talk to her friends about you. And one of those friends may phone you up one day and hire you to do his personal history!

Here are four suggestions that will help you retain a client who can't afford you.

1. Meet the client's budget with an appropriate product.
If your client can only afford $500—not $5,000—then provide a list of things you could do for that fee. You'll have to plan ahead to have a list of lower priced products. Some suggestions: an unedited video or audio recounting of a special event such as a wedding, major travel adventure, or life altering experience.

2. Provide some limited services.
You could offer several coaching sessions to get your client started on writing a life story. Alternatively, you might provide some help starting the person on a DIY family story software program like *Personal Historian*.

3. Offer to find another personal historian.

There are personal historians who are starting out and who need to have samples of work for their portfolio. Some of these individuals might be prepared to offer their services at a modest fee. There are other personal historians for whom the work is largely a hobby. They would likely consider doing the work for little or no money.

4. Provide a list of personal history resources.

For those clients who can't afford anything, provide them with a list of books and web sites that could help them write their own life stories.

74 How to Still be a Winner After Losing a Potential Client

What do you do when you lose a potential client? This happened to me. I was disappointed but it's not the first time and it won't be the last time that I hear the words, "I'm sorry but…" However, over the years I've learned to see this as an opportunity and not as a loss. Let me explain.

I thanked my client for her interest in my services and proposed several inexpensive ideas that could still allow her to capture something of her father's life. I pointed her to a previous blog article of mine, *How to Write Your Life Story in Twenty Statements* (shared in my other book *Skills for Personal Historians*). I suggested this could be a jumping off point for her father to reflect on his journey and document his thoughts with a digital voice recorder.

I also proposed that perhaps a grandchild armed with some questions and a recorder could interview the grandfather and capture something of his story.

I felt better being able to offer some alternatives and she felt good about her experience with me. And that's crucial. While I won't be working with her on this project, who knows what the future holds? Perhaps one day she might want me to document *her* life story. Or she may pass my name on to a friend or colleague who's looking for a personal historian. It's planting seeds that can grow into future work.

So what might you be able to offer potential clients who turn you down? Here are some suggestions for saying, "Thank you for contacting me."

- Provide a list of "How To" books and web resources on recording life stories.
- Give out "50 Best Life Story Questions." (Shared in my other book *Skills for Personal Historians*).
- Provide the names of local personal historians who are starting out and might be willing to work for a lower fee.
- Present a copy of the Association of Personal Historians anthology, *My Words Are Gonna Linger*.
- Provide a book on how to record life stories such as *Legacy: A Step-By-Step Guide to Writing Personal History, How to Write Your Own Life Story*, or *Keeping Family Stories Alive*.
- Give a subscription to a magazine such as *Family Tree Magazine*.

If you put your mind to it, it's not hard to come up with some simple, inexpensive ways to say, "I appreciate your contacting me. I'm sorry we can't work together, but your desire to record your loved one's personal history is important. And I want to honor your commitment."

75 Are You Charging Hamburger Prices for Gourmet Work?

It's not uncommon for those starting out in the personal history business to offer their expertise at rock-bottom rates. And while this might be important for the first project or two, it's definitely not a plan for financial solvency and success in the long run.

How much are you charging per hour for your personal history services?

To give you some idea of where your fees fit with others, I've compiled some lists. From PayScale.com here are the current median average U.S. hourly wages for some different occupations. The figures are based on ten years' experience. Keep in mind these are average wages that vary from state to state and from large metropolitan areas to smaller cities.

- Senior Editor: $29.20.
- Registered Nurse: $25.49.
- Master Plumber: $19.65.
- Writer: $19.64.
- Flight Attendant: $19.33.
- Automotive Service Technician: $15.93.
- Secondary School Teacher: $14.74.
- Computer repair Technician: $12.12.

PoeWar.com lists the average salaries for writers and editors in mid-sized metro areas for 2010. These are not freelance salaries but writers employed by companies. I've converted the annual salaries to hourly rates based on a forty hour week and fifty-two weeks of employment. Here are some of the hourly rates.

- Copy Editor: $10.50 to $21.00.
- Proofreader: $14.50 to $20.50.
- Editor: $18.50 to $27.00.
- Senior Copywriter: $27.00 to $40.00.

Guru.com lists 1,084 creative writing freelancers for New York City. My analysis of the data shows that the majority of these writers charge between $20 and $50 an hour.

I'm not going to tell you how much you should be charging for your services but scanning these lists suggests that anything less than $20 an hour puts you in the hamburger league.

If I haven't yet convinced you of the need to charge a fee commensurate with your skill and the service you provide, then take a look at this interesting bit of research. *Marketing Experiments* in 2004 offered an online book with three different price points: $7.95, $14.00, and $24.95. The cheapest-priced book was perceived as of lesser value and received 1,950 orders for total revenues of $15,500. The $14.00 book had 2,400 orders with revenues of $33,600.

But here's the interesting point. The most expensive book, while receiving only 1,500 orders, managed to make the most: $37,425.

You need to ask yourself, "How can I determine what my market will bear?"

Something else to think about. A Stanford University study showed that when subjects were given the same wine and told that one bottle was $5 and the other $45, people unfailingly found "the expensive wine" tasted better. "So, in essence, [price] is changing people's experiences with a product and, therefore, the outcomes from consuming this product," said Baba Shiv, a professor of marketing who co-authored the research report.

What do these studies say about how you price your personal history services? They show that pricing too low can be perceived by your potential clients as you're offering an inferior product. People still believe the old adage—you get what you pay for.

So when will you start charging gourmet prices for your work?

76 How Much Should You Charge for a Speaking Engagement?

One of the questions I get asked when someone has been invited to give a presentation on personal histories is "How much should I charge?"

Unfortunately, there is no easy answer or formula, but there are some useful guidelines. A colleague of mine, and fellow Association of Personal Historians member, is Pattie Whitehouse. She has some good suggestions that I've summarized below.

If it's a 30-45 minute presentation on personal history and the event is free, don't charge. Consider it part of your marketing. But if you're asked for a full-scale seminar of two to three hours, charge for that. How much, though, will depend on the following:

- How long will it take you to prepare the presentation? You should make preparation time a part of your overall charges.
- Can you market the presentation to other groups? And is this something you'd want to do? If it is, you won't need to put in as much preparation time for future groups. Would this group help you secure other bookings? If the answer is yes to these questions, you might consider reducing your presentation fee.
- How likely is it that you will get business, either directly or indirectly, from your presentation? If likely, you might be willing to charge less; if not likely, you might want to charge what you think you're worth.
- Do you know the group's budget? What have they paid for other presentations? Ask! If their budget is unrealistically low or if they are used to paying a nominal honorarium, you'll need to reconsider. How do you feel, say, about charging a church group less than you might charge a for-profit corporation?

Ultimately, what you charge will come down to a balancing act. You'll need to weigh the experience, the exposure, the raising of awareness about personal history, and the opportunity to present yourself as a knowledgeable professional against the cost to you in time and effort of putting together and making the presentation.

I would add a few other suggestions to Pattie's excellent list:

- When discussing your presentation fee with a non-profit organization, consider quoting your regular fee with a 15% to 25% "non-profit" discount. Doing this honors your professionalism, informs the organization what your actual fee is, and shows your appreciation for its limited funding.

- Factor in your "star" quality when quoting a fee. You won't be in the Bill Gates or Tony Blair league but your years of experience, visibility in your local community, and previous "gigs" all give you some clout when negotiating with an organization.

- Don't forget to factor audience size into your presentation fee. Is this a conference where you're a keynote speaker in front of hundreds or is this a local service club with 50 members? The larger size justifies a higher fee.

- A negotiating line that I like to use sometimes is, "My usual fee is____ but if it's a deal breaker, I'm flexible."

- Consider whether speaking engagements are going to be a major thrust of your personal history work or just an occasional activity. The answer to that will determine how you market yourself and what you charge.

A final word. Appreciate the experience and the value you bring to potential audiences. And never, never, let yourself agree to a deal that doesn't recognize your worth.

77 If You Don't Like What I Charge, Too Bad!

Those of you who followed my blog know that I periodically had the need for a good "old-fashioned" rant. It's kind of therapeutic. And I like to think that perhaps I voice some of the same frustrations that you experience. So hang on to your hat, here's my latest!

I haven't met anyone who doesn't love the idea of a personal history, that is, until they find out how much it costs. Then I usually get looks of incredulity, shock, or disapproval. This is often followed by something like, "I'll have to think about this and get back to you" or "I'm afraid that's much more than we had planned." In any respect, I usually never hear from them again. Now I don't charge outrageous fees. For the most part, they fall within the range charged by other personal historians.

Why is it that as a professional I'm expected to work for "sweat shop" wages? No one for a minute would challenge the rates charged for legal or financial services. And the same people who question my fees think nothing of spending thousands of dollars on renovating their kitchen or bathroom. What gives?

There was a time I used to cringe inwardly when the conversation with a potential client turned to money. Not anymore! I know that I bring years of hard-earned experience to the table. I've won significant awards attesting to the quality of my work and I have many satisfied clients.

Now, when it's time to quote costs, I hold my head high. I look people in the eye and give it to them straight. No tugging at my forelock. No eyes cast downward. No stammering. And if they don't like it, too bad. They can get cousin Harold to do the work. I'm sure he has a little digital video camera and won't charge a cent!

Thank you and have a nice day.

78 Worried About Paying the Bills Between Major Projects?

What do you do when you're between major personal history projects and your bank account is dwindling? If you're like me, this can be a stressful time. One solution is to look for smaller projects that can be done relatively easily and quickly to tide you over. Here are a few things I've done:

- *One-hour audio interviews.* These are delivered unedited on a labeled CD and packaged in a plastic case with generic cover. I let the client choose the topic or suggest possible themes.
- *Transferring old home movies to DVD.* The footage is lightly edited and enhanced.
- *Memorial photo video.* Preparing a collage of photos combined with music that conveys the life story of the deceased.
- *Story editing.* Working with clients to provide some editing to enhance the structure of their personal history.

Depending on your unique set of skills, there are other small projects that you can market. I had the good fortune of attending a workshop called *Small Projects, Steady Income* at an Association of Personal

Historians conference. It was facilitated by Julie McDonald Zander of *Chapters of Life* and Maia Fischler of *LifeWriter*.

Here are a few of their ideas they've kindly allowed me to share:

- Histories of homes and buildings
- A grandparent story-reading or story-telling CD
- History of a family heirloom
- Transcribing/editing diaries
- Scanning of photos and memorabilia
- Cover designs for books, CDs, and DVDs
- Digital photo organization
- Life-writing classes or workshops
- Mother's or Father's Day one-hour interview
- Legacy letter
- Tribute/memorial booklets
- Family reunion booklets and videos
- Recollections for a milestone anniversary or birthday

79 16 Penny-Pinching Ideas to Keep Your Small Business Afloat

Are you struggling to survive in these tough economic times? I've been self-employed for a long time and know what it's like to keep going through lean years. If I've one key piece of advice, it would be to watch the small stuff. You'd be surprised at how a few dollars a week can add up over a year.

Here's are 16 penny-pinching ideas worth trying:

1. Check out thrift stores and garage sales.

Don't spend a fortune on office furnishings. Local thrift stores and garage sales are a good bet for desks, chairs, and filing cabinets. Even better, get stuff free through organizations such as *Freecycle*.

2. Buy used equipment.

I've used refurbished computers for years and been very happy with them. The savings are considerable. Make sure you buy from a reputable dealer who has a warranty on parts and labor.

3. Meet over a coffee rather than lunch.

A few business lunches a year can add up. Your local coffee shop is a more practical alternative. Better yet, invite a client to your home (the coffee's cheaper!).

4. Save on gas.

Consolidate your car trips. If you're driving to pick up groceries, combine it with a trip to the post office, office supply store, or library.

5. Use VoIP.

Don't spend money on long distance calls. Use a VoIP service such as Skype. It's free and easy to set up and use.

6. Become friends with your library.
Stop buying books and magazines and renting DVDs. They're all free at your library.

7. Go online.
Before spending your hard earned dollars, check out the wealth of excellent free resources available on the Internet.

8. Buy only what you absolutely need.
It might be fun to have the latest iPad and smart phone but are they essential items in your business? I'm still using a cell phone I bought 5 years ago. It suits my needs just fine. Don't be seduced into spending money on electronic devices and software that'll do very little to help your business.

9. Be a savvy shopper.
Clip coupons, check out sales, and compare prices. And find out the best time of year to buy things. Here's a start: *The Best Times to Buy Anything, All Year Round* (http://lifehacker.com/5440376/best-time-to-buythe-best-times-to-buy-anything-all-year-round).

10. Negotiate a good deal.
Whether you're dealing with a salesperson or a subcontractor, don't be shy about asking for a discount. I always ask salespeople if that's the best price they can give me. Sometimes paying by cash rather than a credit card will lower the price on an item. With subcontractors, pointing out that you'll be using their services regularly might lead to a reduced fee.

11. Market on the cheap.

This is not the time to be producing glossy brochures and business cards. I've written about some low cost or no cost marketing ideas *25 No Cost or Low Cost Marketing Ideas for Your Personal History Business* (48).

12. Try bartering.

This involves trading goods or services with another business. For example, you might arrange with a web designer to create a website for you. In return, if you're a personal historian, you could organize her photo collection.

13. Monitor your energy consumption.

Shut down your computer when you're not using it for a few hours. Turn off lights that you don't need. And avoid phantom energy loss by literally pulling the plug on all equipment that operates in standby mode such as computers, monitors, computer speakers, and cell phone chargers. Phantom loss can add hundreds of dollars to your yearly electrical bill. To make it easy, plug these standby mode items into a power bar that you can shut off with the flick of a switch.

14. Use tax deductions.

Don't forget that if you're home-based, you can deduct a portion of your rent or mortgage interest. And keep in mind that some of your utilities and home services—such as security, cleaning, and yard maintenance—are eligible for tax deductions.

15. Use recycled printer cartridges.

Printer ink is hugely expensive. Check for a recycle dealer in your area or go to an online source.

16. Consider free web hosting.

It's not perfect but the price is right! For a list of some of the best, check out *Best Free Web Hosting* (http://www.ironspider.ca/website/freewebhost2.htm).

80 News Flash! Being Relaxed Makes People Spend More Freely

A recent issue of the *Journal of Marketing Research* examined the correlation between relaxation and consumer spending. It turns out that, all things being equal, consumers are more willing to pay higher prices if they feel relaxed.

It's no surprise then that we find luxury products typically displayed in high-end boutiques that ooze comfort and elegance. Commenting on the research, *Wired Magazine* wrote:

> *Why does relaxation turn us into spendthrifts? When we feel safe, we are better able to fully focus on the potential rewards at stake. Instead of worrying about price, we can contemplate the advantages of having a sophisticated camera, or the thrill of falling through the air. As the psychologists demonstrated in subsequent experiments, those subjects who were more relaxed thought less about*

particulars—the specific cost of the gadget or the dangers of the risky behavior—and more about the abstract pleasures they were trying to purchase.

What has all this to do with personal historians?

We are in the business of providing a high-end product. Asking individuals to part with $10,000 or more for a personal history requires more from us than offering up a good resume, a nice smile, and an attractive brochure.

If, as the research suggests, a relaxed personal history client is more likely to say yes to a life story, shouldn't we be looking at ways we can enhance the "relaxation" factor?

Here are some ideas worth considering:

Website

Take a look at *Dolce & Gabbana* for some clues on how a high-end retailer provides a very subdued and relaxed online presence. Now examine your website. Is it friendly, inviting, and easy to navigate? Are the colors and photographs calming? Does it offer free resources? Does it have space to breathe? Does the copy tell a heart-warming story? In other words, does it feel relaxed? If you've said yes to all these, then you've made a good start. If not, then you've got some work to do.

Brochures

As with your website design, similar rules apply to your brochure—easy on the eye, inviting, and friendly. Also check out the feel of your brochure. Is it silky smooth and durable like an expensive art card? Avoid stock that's flimsy and feels cheap.

Setting

If possible, choose to meet clients in a calm, relaxing setting. A good choice is often the client's home. People are usually at ease in their own place (unless it's crawling with rambunctious kids and pets).

If you can't meet in a client's home, consider a location that's subdued and attractive such as a boutique bakery, café, a quiet corner of an elegant hotel lobby, or perhaps even your own home.

Appearance

If you're hungry for a contract, you're going to be telegraphing this regardless of your outward expression. A look of desperation in your eyes does nothing to put potential clients at ease.

A more relaxing approach is to assume nothing and make the meeting an opportunity to learn more about your client's wishes. Go with the idea of helping this person realize their personal history project even if it doesn't in the long run involve working with you.

Trust

We know from experience that trusting someone puts us in a more relaxed frame of mind. I've written about this in *3 Keys to Creating Trust with Potential Clients* (36).

Conclusion

As personal historians we need to judiciously apply all the marketing techniques at our disposal in order to reach potential clients and gain their confidence.

The "relaxation" factor isn't a magic bullet. But combined with other marketing approaches it can give you an added advantage.

81 The Costliest Personal Histories in the World!

How many of you would have the nerve to proclaim, "We will *not* be oversold"? Yet that's just what designer and retailer Bijan Pakzad did. For thirty-five years he reigned over his exclusive Rodeo Drive establishment in Los Angeles.

From his by-appointment-only boutique to his claim as "the most expensive clothing designer in the world," Bijan was an unapologetic promoter of exclusivity.

You might be asking yourself, "But what does opulence and exclusivity have to do with personal histories?" Good question, and here's where I see the connection.

People buy products for their perceived benefits not for their features or functions. We purchase a computer not for its technical specifications but for its benefit to us—namely fast research capabilities, entertainment, communications, marketing, and so on. Bijan wasn't selling clothes. He was selling celebrity, exclusivity, and glamour.

As personal historians what are we selling? If you said books, videos, or CDs, you'd be wrong. Those are the products of our work. What people are buying are:

- *Time.* People are busy and don't have the time to document their mom's or dad's story.
- *Satisfaction.* People feel good honoring someone through a life storybook or video.
- *Expertise.* Generally people aren't skilled in the many aspects of producing a personal history and need our help.
- *Closeness.* People perceive that a personal history will bring families closer together.
- *Understanding.* Participating in the recording of a life story gives people a better understanding of who someone is and how that person got to be that way.

People will pay a premium price for specialty products and services. The truth is that while Bijan's clothes are priced at the high end of the designer market at $1,000 for suits, they are hardly the most expensive in the world. The cachet of exclusivity and pampered service draws his clients.

On a more pedestrian level, Starbucks pioneered the brewing of premium coffee in North America. Before Starbucks opened in Seattle in 1971, a cup of coffee was just a cup of coffee and could be had for 10 to 15 cents. Many a skeptic would have questioned the wisdom of charging ten times that amount for a "fancy" coffee. They were proved wrong. The story of Starbucks success is now part of pop culture history.

Personal historians provide a specialty service and product. Like Bijan and Starbucks, we need not apologize for charging a premium price.

I'm not suggesting that every personal historian should sell exclusive products at eye-popping prices. What I do want to emphasize is that we need a shift from seeing ourselves solely as "craftspeople" toiling away in obscurity for the love of our work. That's okay if you're into this as a hobby. It's not okay if you want to build a successful business.

So, who will proudly proclaim that they produce the costliest personal histories in the world?

CHAPTER 7:
Taking Care of Yourself

82 How to Stop the Clock And Make Time for Yourself

If you're self-employed as I am, you're probably all too familiar with the trap of filling most of your days with work. There are deadlines to meet, marketing activities, clients to see, and administrative chores.

Maybe you've found a way to manage all this and still have a life. If you haven't, here are some lessons learned from my three decades of experience that you might find helpful. To be honest, sometimes I "mess up" and don't follow my own guidelines. But they've become a habit now and so it's easier to get back on track when I've run amok.

Take mini breaks.

Taking breaks restores your energy and helps prevent repetitive stress injuries. I take at least four or five breaks during my day. I stop for a 15-

minute cup of tea around 10 am after putting in an hour or more of work. I break for lunch and have a power nap afterwards—no more than 30 minutes, otherwise I feel groggy. Mid-afternoon, I stop for 30 minutes, make some tea (You can tell I like tea!) and read the newspaper. Between 4:30 pm or 5 pm I go for a brisk 30-minute walk. I get back and work until 7 pm. Then I stop for the day.

Make a date with yourself.

I found that unless I actually designated a day free from work and other chores, I never really managed to take time off. So I looked at my work and social demands and decided that Mondays worked best for me. Now here's the trick. This is a day you designate just for you. It's not a time to do all the chores around the house that you've been neglecting. I use my day for play and relaxation. I may read, go for a long walk, check out my favorite Thrift Stores, or putter in the garden.

Begin your day unrushed and peacefully.

I take about two hours from the time I get up until I sit down to work. My day starts (after I feed our cat, Annie) with 30 minutes of meditation. This is followed by about thirty-five minutes of stretching and strengthening exercises. I stop for breakfast, clean up the dishes, and then have a shower. No matter what my day holds for me, I know that starting it off in a calm and peaceful manner means I can cope with almost anything.

Fix a definite time to end your workday.

For years I've made a rule that at 7 p.m. I stop work. I get up and walk away from my desk. I don't take calls unless it's an emergency. If you don't discipline yourself to stop work at a fixed time each day, the danger is that you end up working until you collapse into your bed.

Set boundaries and keep to them.

If you're unclear what boundaries are important to you, chances are you'll get blown about like a leaf in a storm. I've alluded to some of my boundaries above. I end my day at 7 p.m. There has to be a very compelling reason to change that. Monday is my free day. Nothing interrupts that unless it's a call from the President of the United States! And that has yet to happen. There are other boundaries you can set that have to do with your fees, the quality of work you expect from yourself and others, the type of personal history project you won't undertake, and so on.

83 The Power of "No"

> *Saying "no" politely is a necessity if one wants to lead any kind of stable life.* ~ Richard Chamberlain

The "N" word has a bad reputation. It's seen as negative and mean. Many of us find it hard to say. But saying *No* will help you not only with your work as a personal historian but also with your life in general. I'm getting better at saying *No* but there's room for improvement.

The reality is that saying *No* is a healthy way of providing us with the space we need to be the best we can be. Saying *No* takes back control of our lives. You have a right to say *No* and feel good about it. Here are ten things where *No* can be the answer. Do you have any to add to the list?

No to clutter.
Physical and mental clutter fills space and leaves us less energy for the things we really want to do. Clean up your office and throw stuff out. Being mindful of the moment and focusing on one thing at a time will reduce mental clutter.

No to worry.

> *"I worry about scientists discovering that lettuce has been fattening all along."* ~ Erma Bombeck

So what are you worrying about? Can you do something about it? Then do it. Action is a powerful antidote to worry. If your worry is something you can't do anything about, then let it go. For every minute spent worrying we could spend that minute reflecting on the good in our lives. The mind can't hold two thoughts at the same time. Hold thoughts that are pleasing. Soon there will be little space for worry!

No to the Gremlin.
Our Inner Critic keeps us locked in old beliefs and time worn patterns. Recognizing our Gremlins and saying *No* to them opens up new ways of interacting with the world.

No to procrastination.
When we think of tasks as difficult or inconvenient, there's a tendency to procrastinate. When we give in to procrastination, we perform poorly and are often under increased stress. One solution: break big tasks into small size pieces.

No to time wasters.
How is your time wasted during the day? Make a list of all the situations that waste your time and then zap them! You know what they are—answering solicitation calls, listening to gossip, trying to find that document you filed somewhere, surfing the Internet, and grocery shopping at the busiest time of the day.

No to overwhelm.
Taking on one more task or project can tip us into overwhelm. Ask what you will have to say *No* to before saying yes to your next project.

No to pleasing people all the time.

> *"I really cannot give you the formula for success. But I can give you the formula for failure. It's this: try to please everyone."* ~ Bernard Meltzer

We all want to be liked. For some of us that means saying yes to everyone so that they'll like us. It's a no-win situation. You can't please everyone all the time and so someone is bound to feel slighted. It's better to be clear about who has a priority on your time and be generous to those people than to stretch yourself thinly and satisfy no one.

No to tolerations.
Our lives are full of things that we tolerate. They sap our energy and limit our potential. Tolerations can be big and small from tolerating an unhappy relationship to tolerating a squeaky door. Limit your tolerations and you'll have more room in your life.

No to blame.

Blaming others for our difficulties is not helpful. A better approach is to examine your strengths. Then ask yourself, "How can I use my strengths to improve my business and my life?"

No to "toxic" clients.

You don't want to be around clients for whom nothing is right. You may think that you need every client you can lay your hands on but you can do better. Fire your "toxic" client and you'll leave an opening for someone who really values your services.

84 10 Tips on Creating a Pain Free Work Space

A good deal of my time is spent hunched over my computer either video editing or working on print documents. My posture leaves something to be desired.

For years I've been able to get away with poor posture. Not anymore. I've been forced by a painful right shoulder blade and hip to monitor more closely how I arrange my chair, desk, and computer. If you're beginning to develop some aches and pains from working at your computer, keep on reading!

I researched several websites on workplace ergonomics and boiled down their information into these ten tips.

1. Your keyboard should be tilted slightly away from you and positioned just above your lap so that your arms are parallel to your thighs or slope slightly downward.
2. Your wrists should be in a neutral or unbent position, not resting on the desk or a wrist support.
3. Your shoulders should be relaxed and your arms close to your body.
4. Your mouse should be held lightly and positioned close to your keyboard to avoid over reaching.
5. Your monitor should be directly in front of you and about arm's length away.
6. Your monitor should be placed to minimize glare from a window.
7. Your monitor should be positioned so that your eye level is about 2 to 3 inches below the top of the monitor.
8. Your monitor should tilt back slightly.
9. Your chair should be adjustable, have lumbar support, and arm rests.
10. Your feet should be flat on the floor with your thighs pointing slightly downward.

In addition, it's also important to make sure you get up from your desk at least every 30 minutes and do some stretches. You might want to try *The Ultimate "Deskercise" Stretch Routine* (http://www.health-line.com/health-slideshow/deskercise).

There's no excuse for me now. I'll just have to put all these tips into practice. But I need prompting. I've found a web meditation timer that

I've set to chime every 15 minutes. This reminds me to check my posture.

85 Creating the Spaciousness You Want in Your Life

Are you feeling harried, with no time for yourself, and overwhelmed by too much stuff? Imagine what it would be like to enter a place of spaciousness where calmness, openness, and deep satisfaction prevailed. It's not impossible. Let me explain.

At the beginning of the year I wrote about my intentions. One of my intentions was to create more spaciousness in my life.

Here's what I've done so far. It's still a work in progress but here are some thoughts on creating your own spaciousness.

Begin with the mind.
Creating spaciousness in the mind is a start.

I've been practicing Insight Meditation for the past 15 years. I realized that while my 30 minutes a day was better than nothing, it wasn't sufficient to settle my "monkey mind."

I've added a second 30-minute mediation session at the end of my work day before dinner. I'm finding that my mindfulness is better and I don't feel as rushed. The simple act of carving out meditation time in my day has forced me to slow down. The mind feels more spacious.

Here's my suggestion. Start a simple meditation practice. At first it can be just ten minutes a day. The important thing is to get into the habit of doing it. Be patient. It takes time for habits to take hold. If you need some suggestions for meditation practice, check these out:

- *Meditation for Beginners* (http://tinyurl.com/26zpoob)
- *Insight Meditation Instruction* [Audio] (http://tinyurl.com/lujbaxf)

Learn to say "No."

I've written about the power of "No" in *The Power of "No"* (83). It's taken me time but I'm much better at protecting my space by using that one simple word. I'm also aware that as an introvert I need my downtime. Friends have come to respect the fact that I seldom do parties.

If you want to carve out some space for yourself, you need to be able to say "No" and not feel guilty about it.

Schedule "spaciousness."

No one is going to give you time. You've got to make it happen. I discovered that unless I actually built free time into my daily and weekly schedule it too easily got used up with busyness. Now I've built a "fire wall" around my evenings and early mornings. And I've set aside several days in the week that are non-work, free space times to do as I wish.

I suggest you start by looking at where you can block out periods of time that are just for you. Schedule them into your day planner and be resolute about keeping those dates.

Get rid of "stuff."

Stuff to me is anything that's filling my space and that doesn't have some decorative or practical purpose.

I'm not a "neat freak" and I can live with a certain amount of clutter. The problem is that I've got too much stuff that has no purpose.

I've started a methodical process of sorting through my stuff. I'm removing titles from the bookshelves that I'm never going to read again. I'm donating magazine back-issues to the local library. I've got a box that I'm filling with knickknacks for the Hospice Thrift Boutique. There are dated and dead electronic devices that I'm sending to be recycled.

Look around you. What's the stuff in your life? Start small by dedicating some time each week to eliminating items and opening up your work and living space.

86 Stop Struggling and Succeed!

I spent a recent weekend on a silent Buddhist Insight Meditation retreat. I've been practicing Insight Meditation regularly for over a decade and twice a year I attend a two-day retreat. It's hard work and useful insights arise.

The most useful is the discovery that forcing yourself to be calm only makes the mind and body more tense. Struggling doesn't work. It's like training a dog to "stay." It requires patience. You can't force it. You have to gently and repeatedly bring the dog back, sit it down, and tell it to "stay." Eventually it catches on. The mind works the same way. In order to change old ways or learn new ones we need commitment, practice, and patience.

This got me thinking that too often we fail to succeed in our work and life, not because we don't try hard enough but that we try too hard. When we struggle, we eventually get burned out, discouraged, and give up or look for magical solutions. So how can we apply the wisdom of Insight Meditation in a practical way to our work? Here's a six-step approach you might try:

1. Write down a goal you want to achieve.

Remember to make your goal S.M.A.R.T. i.e., Specific, Measurable, Attainable, Realistic, and Timely or Tangible. For example, you might write down: *I will increase the number of people receiving my newsletter by 10% by [insert date].* Now commit yourself to this goal. It helps to make it public. Tell your friends, colleagues, and partner the goal you've set for yourself.

2. Determine the next step.

I suggest using the *Getting Things Done* method pioneered by David Allen. Determine each action needed to get one step closer to completing your goal. Using the example above you might write down as your first step: *Google "how to newsletter marketing."* The second next step could be: *Identify three articles and bookmark them.* The third step: *Read the three articles.*

3. Set up a schedule.

Make a commitment to complete at least one action step a day. Mark a specific time in your calendar that you'll do this work. By completing a task a day you're in effect training your mind to work in a systematic, scheduled, and productive manner. It's like the dog training analogy.

4. Be patient.

This is really important. There are going to be times when life gets in the way and you can't complete one of your daily action steps. Don't beat yourself up over this. Acknowledge that other priorities have made it impossible to work on your goal and commit yourself to picking up where you left off the next day. Likewise, you may find that you have to go back and repeat some action steps before moving on. That's okay. As long as you've made a commitment to reaching your goal, you'll get there.

5. Check for signs of struggle.

If you're like me, it's easy to fall into struggling. It tends to be my default position. Here are some common warning signs that you're into struggle. Your energy level drops at about the same time as you begin your scheduled task. Your inner critic begins to sow doubt. It says things like, "This is a waste of time. Who told you that you could achieve this goal? You'll never be successful." You become more easily annoyed. You lose interest in your work. Nothing seems to be working as you've planned.

6. Avoid struggling.

First, be aware of the warning signs so that you can pull back. Next, ask yourself if you've been trying too hard. Maybe an action step each day is too much given your schedule. If so, plan a routine that works better. Make sure to acknowledge each of the steps you complete. Note that you're moving steadily toward your goal, one small step at a time. Take a break. Forget about your goal and your action steps for a short time. Do something that you know relaxes you.

I believe that if you apply commitment, practice, and patience without struggle your chances of success in all that you do are more likely.

87 Stop With the Productivity Pitches!

> *I took a speed-reading course and read War and Peace in twenty minutes. It involves Russia.* ~ Woody Allen

Google "personal productivity" and out gush 102,000 blogs and 2,440,000 articles. Among them you can learn 15 Ways to Maximize Your Lunch Hour. Call me crazy but I like a quiet lunch followed by a nap. If I want to maximize anything, it's a longer siesta!

One productivity guru promises that you too can *Live A Stress Free Life With Time Management*. Really? If it were that easy, the sales of Ativan would plummet.

My beef with the cult of productivity is that it implies that through increased efficiency we'll get more done, have more free time, and be happier. It feeds on our desire to have it all.

News Flash! Happiness can't be achieved through productivity.

Don't get me wrong. Productivity has its place as long as it doesn't become an end in itself. Spending our days checking things off lists, getting things done, and measuring our progress won't ultimately make us happier or our business more successful.

Here's a modest proposal. Rather than being caught up in the productivity game, just give up! That's right. Give up.

Let me illustrate with a personal example. Some years ago I decided to transition out of documentary filmmaking and become a life coach. I enrolled with the Coaches Training Institute and after a rigorous year graduated as a Certified Professional Co-Active Coach.

I worked hard for the first couple of years marketing, honing my skills, and building a small client base. One day it dawned on me that I really wasn't happy spending my time on a telephone coaching clients. No amount of increased efficiency was going to change that fact. So I gave up coaching. It wasn't easy but I needed to move on. I'm glad I did.

Giving up means acceptance of things as they are. It means stopping the constant need to change things. As "crazy" as it sounds, giving up will ultimately make you happier and your work more joyful.

What can you give up? Here are some suggestions to get you started:

- Give up being super productive
- Give up trying to be perfect
- Give up trying to be all things to all people
- Give up worrying about the competition
- Give up working 12 hour days
- Give up working at happiness
- Give up all the "stuff" that's useless
- Give up toxic acquaintances
- Give up trying to be #1

- Give up the self-improvement merry-go-round

Woody Allen's humorous take on speed-reading gets at the heart of an obsession with productivity. In our drive for ever-increasing efficiency we rob ourselves of life's very essence.

What do you think? What are you prepared to give up?

88 Shut Down Your Computer!

If you're like most personal historians, you spend a lot of time in front of a computer screen. I certainly do. Lately, I've come across information that suggests that I need to shut off my computer and get outside. In fact, if I don't, it could kill me!

A Swedish study reported in the *British Journal of Sports Medicine* suggests that prolonged sitting can lead to cancer, obesity, diabetes, and heart disease. While this isn't earth-shattering news, the discovery that no amount of exercise eradicates this risk certainly was.

A similar Canadian study published last year tracked more than 17,000 people for an average of twelve years. It also found that exercising had no effect on reducing health risks in sedentary people. Clearly, if I want to live longer, I'd better get up from my computer more often and start moving!

If that's not convincing enough, here's another reason to unplug your computer. This week I came across an article in *The Harvard Business Review,* "For Real Productivity, Less is Truly More." The author Tony Schwartz argues quite persuasively that working ten or twelve-hour days is counterproductive. What we need to be doing is following our natural ultradian rhythms. This is a cycle that runs from higher to lower mental alertness every 90 minutes throughout the day. Schwartz says we should take meaningful breaks after every 90 minutes of work. He himself has a routine that schedules him to have breakfast after his first 90 minutes, jog after his second, and lunch after his third. It makes sense to work this way. It's how athletes train. They work hard in short bursts and then rest. So for me, no more sitting glued to my computer for a couple of hours without a break.

Finally, I've started to read "You Are Not a Gadget" by Jaron Lanier, the father of virtual reality technology. Lanier's provocative book is a passionate call to reclaim our individual humanity from the anonymous hive-mind of the digital world. Beware of "cybernetic totalism," he warns. I'm only a third of the way through the book and already I'm beginning to look at social networking with a much more critical eye.

Well, enough for today. I'm shutting down my computer and going for a good brisk walk. I'll drink deeply of the sweet spring air, talk to the odd neighborhood cat, and smile at strangers.

CLICK!

89 Are You Part of "The Great Vacationless Class?"

Anne Morrow Lindbergh observed that, for the most part, mothers and housewives were the "great vacationless class" because they had little time off. I would add the self-employed to her list.

If you're self-employed as I am, it's often difficult to see your way to a holiday. You're either too busy or too broke or both.

Here are a few tips that you might find useful if you're still struggling with the notion of taking a vacation.

Silence the "Gremlins."
As soon as I think or say "vacation", my inner critics start whispering. *That's irresponsible. People depend on you. Your business will fail. You'll lose clients!* Gremlins want to keep the status quo. You need to recognize these voices for what they are and politely tell them to "Get lost." If you don't, you'll end up chained to your desk.

Plan ahead and set firm dates.
Setting dates forces you to make a commitment. It's critical to allow yourself several weeks lead time. The more the better. This allows you to wrap up projects or stages of a project. Don't cram everything into the final week before your vacation. You'll end up exhausted and won't enjoy your time off. Make sure that you don't plan any project work the week you return. This will allow you to settle in and catch up on e-mails and other administrative matters.

Inform your current clients.

Don't try to pretend that you're still at your desk. Letting clients know of your vacation avoids the embarrassment of their trying to reach you and not getting a reply for a couple of weeks. Trust that your clients understand that you're human and like everyone else need some free time.

Set up an e-mail auto-responder.

Even though you're having a "staycation," resist the temptation to peek at e-mails. Leave an auto-responder message that goes something like, "Thank you for contacting me. I'm currently away from my desk and unavailable from August 21st until September 5th. I'll answer your e-mail on my return. If this is an emergency, please call 250-514-****."

Leave a vacation voice-message on your answering service.

Even if you're staying close to home on your vacation, you don't want the interruption of business calls. Add a telephone message that says something like, "Thanks for calling. I'm away from my desk until September 5th. Please leave a message and I'll be happy to return your call when I'm back. If this is an emergency, please call 250-514-****." A word of caution. It's advisable in both your e-mail and telephone messages not to give the impression that you've left your home or office vacant. This information could fall into the wrong hands and lead to a robbery.

Relax.

It sounds obvious. But if you're like me, you probably have what I'd call the "Manager of the Universe" syndrome. It goes, "The world will stop spinning on its axis if I'm not at my desk 24/7." Well I know and you know that's ridiculous. It's quite amazing how the world keeps turning even when we're not involved. So, give yourself permission not to worry and just relax.

90 The Secret to a Successful "Staycation"

The wag who said the alternative to a vacation is to stay home and tip every third person you see had a point. Vacations can be expensive and exhausting. There's airport gridlock, cramped planes, missed connections, lost baggage, upset digestion, poor sleep, and oh yes, tipping!

But if your vacation at home is to be refreshing and a break from routine, it requires a little thought and planning. Here's the secret to a successful staycation.

Turn off your work mind.
I know it's easier said than done. What you have to do is stop yourself from planning or in any other way obsessing about your work. My default position is planning. I do it in my sleep. So what I need to do is catch myself thinking about work and tell myself quite forcefully, "STOP!" It'll take some time before my mind catches on but it will. Repeat after me, "I'm not the Center of the Universe. It will continue without me and my planning."

Walk away from your computer.
If you spend, as I do, a lot of time staring at a computer screen, turning it off can be like kicking an addiction. Checking on e-mails and your

Twitter and Facebook friends is not a holiday. If you absolutely must look at your Inbox, make it once a day. Preferably, choose the beginning of the day. Then it's out of the way and you can get on with your holiday.

Set up an e-mail auto-respond message.

To assist in your computer withdrawal, post an auto-respond message that tells people you're away and when you'll be back to answer their messages. If you feel the need, you can always leave an emergency telephone number.

Don't answer your telephone.

Answering business calls is not a holiday. Record an outgoing message that lets clients know you're unavailable and that you'll get back to them when you return.

Get out of the house.

If you work from home, this is an absolute necessity. Here are some ideas. Pack a picnic lunch, invite a friend, and find a quiet park or beach. Pretend you're a tourist and visit places that you've wanted to see but never had the time. Visit a museum or art gallery. Take in a musical concert, stage play, or dance production.

Plan some home time.

Make sure that all your days aren't spent running around. Take time at home to read, watch some good movies, listen to your favorite music, take naps, and generally "veg out." Don't use your home time to catch up on neglected chores, like cleaning out the garage or washing the windows. That isn't a holiday.

Splurge.

You're not spending a small fortune on a vacation so why not indulge in a few treats? Here are a few suggestions—a massage session, a house cleaning service, a dinner at an upscale restaurant, a night at a fancy hotel, a day at a spa, a catered meal at home, a box of decadent chocolates. You get the idea.

91 My "Staycation." Would I Do It Again?

I took a two-week break at home, following the advice I gave in the previous tip (see 90: The Secret to a Successful "Staycation").

Here's some added advice based on my recent experience.

Be prepared for surprises and move on.

These can be both good and bad. Mine were of the bad variety. Two days before my planned break my computer broke down. By the time I'd looked into repairing it, decided not to do so, bought a new computer, and caught up on the work I needed to do before taking off, my two weeks was reduced to ten days. But I still made the most of the time left.

Be flexible.

I know that in my previous article on "staycations" I wrote about getting away from your computer. I decided that I needed to check my e-mails twice a day. Once in the morning and once at night. I didn't want to have hundreds of e-mail messages piled up when I got back. This worked for me. But it did take a conscious effort to stay away from my computer. There was the temptation to hang around and do more.

Adjust your expectations.

Before my break I'd built up in my mind an impressive list of things I was going to do. Truth is I would have needed a month to accomplish everything. So I pared away at my list. I focused on a few things I really wanted to do, like taking a day trip by ferry to Vancouver and seeing an old friend.

Shake up routines.

Because my life tends to be heavily scheduled, I wanted to avoid programming every minute of my holiday. Some of my favorite times were spent sitting on my back patio doing nothing but watching the birds at the feeder and the clouds drifting by.

Accept that a "staycation" is a break, not a holiday.

If you expect that your "staycation" will give you the same feeling of escape and adventure as a trip away, you'll be disappointed. I had hoped for more. But on reflection, I realize that I was able to take enough of a break that I feel ready to plunge into a very busy fall.

Would I do it again? The answer is definitely yes. But given what I've learned, I'd adjust some of my plans and expectations.

92 What Tony Bennett Can Teach Us About Burnout

Tony Bennett is an inspiration. Besides his album *Viva Duets* and memoir *Life is a Gift*, Bennett continues to tour. How does he do all this without getting burnt out? The answer comes in an interview he gave Jacob Richler in *Zoomer* magazine. He said:

> *As soon as you get burnt out singing, you go over to painting. As soon as you get burned out painting, you go back to singing—and it feels new again, every time. Maybe if you just did one thing, eventually you'd say to yourself, 'I've got to take a vacation and get away from this.' I never feel burnt out. To me, I'm on perpetual vacation. I'm very fortunate.*

How can we put these wise words into practice in our own lives?

First we need to be aware of the signs of burnout. These include exhaustion, emotional numbness, lack of motivation, hopelessness, depression, and disengagement. Many of us have been there at some time in our working lives. That's why people opt out of the "rat race" and become self-employed in professions like personal history.

But being self-employed and running a personal history business is no guarantee that we won't get burnt out. In fact being passionate about our work can unwittingly draw us into bad habits—neglecting exercise, meals grabbed on the run, late nights, no down time, and over-commitment.

What Bennett is saying about avoiding burnout is that we need to take a complete break from what we're doing and focus on something entirely different.

Here's how to put Bennett's prescription into practice:

Make a "joy" list.
Write down all the things you like doing that bring you joy and make you happy. For me it can be as simple as a walk along a beach or a quiet hour reading.

Schedule "joy."
It may sound strange but if you don't schedule in your "joyful" activities, it's too easy to fill your time with more work. Take your list and build some joyful moments into your daily and weekly schedule. I always make time in the morning to do thirty minutes of meditation followed by forty minutes of stretching exercises. Now I know that not everyone would consider that joyful!

Take a vacation.
Plan a minimum of a week to get away from your office. Unplug from your wired universe. Leave behind your laptop and avoid checking e-mails on your smart phone. Even if you can't get away from your home, you can take a "Staycation." I wrote about this in another article (90: *The Secret to a Successful "Staycation"*).

Establish boundaries.
Learn to say "No." Saying "Yes" all the time will erode more and more of your precious downtime. Check out *The Power of "No"* (83) for more on how to say "No."

Switch tasks.
Pablo Picasso avoided burnout by making sure that his studio held an array of different projects. All were in various stages of completion and all within sight. When he got frustrated or bored with a project he could

simply turn and pick one of his many others. Like Tony Bennett, variety kept him fresh. You can do the same thing by having a range of appealing tasks that are easily accessible and not time-sensitive. Feeling overwhelmed and tired? Just switch to something else.

Acknowledgments

THIS BOOK WOULD NOT have been possible without the help of the following people: first and foremost Jim Osborne, my life partner and writing mentor who painstakingly copyedited every post in my original blog; Kathleen McGreevy at Chapter Savers who did a great job as editor, categorizing and arranging all of my blog posts into a coherent book; Monica Lee at Clickago Storywerks who formatted the ebook and paperback and designed an eye-catching cover; Sarah White, APH President, and the APH Board, who approached me with the idea of converting my blog posts into a book; Linda Coffin, APH Executive Director, who carefully shepherded the project along; and all my regular blog readers who encouraged me and made it a delight to write for them. Thank you.

About the Author

DAN CURTIS IS AN award-winning documentary filmmaker, writer, certified life coach, and professional personal historian. He lives in Victoria, British Columbia.

If you enjoyed this book, please consider leaving a review at Amazon, even it's only a line or two. It helps get the word out about the profession of Personal Historians and would be very much appreciated.

Sample of
Skills for Personal Historians

WANT MORE IDEAS? AUTHOR Dan Curtis also wrote *Skills for Personal Historians: 102 Savvy Ideas to Boost Your Expertise,* filled with suggestions and lessons drawn from his years of experience in the field of helping others tell their life stories. Here's a sample:

The #1 Secret to a Successful Life Story Interview

Picture this. You sit down to conduct a personal history interview. You pull out your voice recorder and your client looks stricken. You reassure her that there's no need to worry and ask your first question. She looks at the floor and gives a brief two or three word response. It doesn't get any better. It feels as though your "pulling teeth." Beads of perspiration break out on your forehead. You finish the interview and leave for home, tired and discouraged.

What went wrong?

Some of you will say it was the voice recorder that made the client uneasy. Nope! Not the recorder. Today's devices are small and unobtrusive. There might be some initial discomfort but it passes—like gas. I've done hundreds of hours of interviews and within a few minutes people forget there's even a recorder in the room. So don't blame the recorder.

Sorry to say but the problem rests with the interviewer. If you're not comfortable with the equipment or anxious about getting a good interview or worried about the questions you're going to ask, then your anxiety is going to rub off on your client. Neuroscience research has uncovered "mirror neurons" which seems to indicate that if we see someone frowning or smiling, it triggers a similar internal reaction in us.

In a word, the #1 secret to a successful interview is *rapport*. Here's what you need to do.

Before the interview, make your initial visit a "get-to-know."

Nothing creates more anxiety in a client than rushing in all "business-like," ready to record. Take an hour to have a conversation with your client. Stress the personal. Imagine you're dropping in on a favorite aunt or uncle. Do talk about the upcoming interview but spend as much time if not more on small talk.

I try to get a quick sense of people's interests by looking at how they've decorated and what treasures they've chosen to display. A question about a painting, photo, or figurine can unlock some charming stories. And it puts your client at ease. Find something in common—maybe it's grandchildren, a favorite author, or similar childhood roots.

Arrive for the interview rested, mindful, focused, and calm.

Remember that clients will pick up on your anxiety. This in turn makes them anxious. When you walk through the door to a client's home, you want to be smiling and aware of what is happening from moment to moment. To do that effectively, you need to be rested and focused solely on the interview at hand. How does your client look? How are you feeling? What extraneous activities or sounds are intruding on your interview space?

Before the interview begins, start with some small talk.

I never set up my recorder or camera for an interview without first engaging my client in some small talk. It can be about the weather, their day or week's activities, or any other subject that's informal. I find a sense of humor and some laughter go a long way to defuse anxiety. I'm also mindful that we've a job at hand and I don't let the chatting eat up too much time.

Set up the recording equipment with practiced nonchalance.

Don't make setting up your recording equipment a "big production." The more I consciously avoid flailing about with my recorder and microphone, the less distressing it is for my client. This means you have to know your equipment superbly. It's not the time to begin fretting over what folder you're recording in or why you're not getting sound in your headphones. It also helps to keep some chit-chat going while you clip on a lavaliere mic and adjust the sound levels.

Rapport. That's the secret.

Want to learn more secrets like this?

Get *Skills for Personal Historians:*
102 Savvy Ideas to Boost Your Expertise

available from the Association of Personal Historians store:
http://store.personalhistorians.org/
and at major booksellers.

Made in the USA
San Bernardino, CA
06 October 2015